Amazon Sumerian User Guide

A catalogue record for this book is available from the Hong Kong Public Libraries.

Published in Hong Kong by Samurai Media Limited.

Email: info@samuraimedia.org

ISBN 9789888408801

Contents

Amazon Sumerian User Guide

A catalogue record for this book is available from the Hong Kong Public Libraries.

Published in Hong Kong by Samurai Media Limited.

Email: info@samuraimedia.org

ISBN 9789888408801

What Is Amazon Sumerian?

Amazon Sumerian is a set of tools for creating high-quality virtual reality (VR) experiences on the web. With Sumerian, you can construct an interactive 3D scene without any programming experience, test it in the browser, and publish it as a website that is immediately available to users.

Use the Sumerian library of assets or bring your own. When you import 3D models, Sumerian converts and optimizes them automatically. Sumerian also has a library of primitive shapes, 3D models, hosts, textures, and scripts.

Note
New to 3D, VR, animation, and scripting? The Sumerian website has a ton of helpful tutorials for every level of experience.

The Sumerian 3D engine provides a library for advanced scripting with JavaScript, but you don't have to be a programmer to create interactive VR! Use the built-in state machine to animate objects and respond to user actions like clicks and movement.

When you're ready to share your work with the world, you can publish it directly to Amazon CloudFront as a static website that can be viewed with a WebVR-compatible browser and headset.

Amazon Sumerian Use Cases and Requirements

At the core of Amazon Sumerian is a web-based editor for constructing 3D scenes with animation, scripted interaction, and special effects. The editor runs in your web browser, and all of your data is stored in AWS. The editor outputs scenes to Amazon CloudFront as a static website that you can load directly into any WebVR-compatible browser and headset, or embed in your website for others to access.

Note

Don't know how to script? The Sumerian editor provides a fully featured state machine for scripting animations and user interactions visually, with no coding required.

WebVR is an open specification that lets you create and share virtual reality (VR) experiences through the web. WebVR applications, like any web app, are supported on several desktop and mobile operating systems. This enables you to avoid the need to port your application to different programming languages and package formats to reach all users. Sumerian provides tools and components that you can use to add VR to your scene.

Sumerian also lets you create augmented reality (AR) applications. An AR application can use your phone's camera or an AR-compatible headset to overlay graphics on the real world. Sumerian provides a template and sample application for creating ARKit applications for iOS phones.

Sumerian provides a library of optimized 3D objects and scene templates that you can use to construct scenes without any existing assets. If you do have 3D models, you can import them with their animations and textures by dragging them from your file system into the editor canvas. Sumerian supports models in OBJ and FBX formats.

Amazon Sumerian Permissions

You can use AWS Identity and Access Management (IAM) to grant Sumerian permissions to users and compute resources in your account. IAM controls access to AWS at the API level to enforce permissions uniformly and securely.

IAM Managed Policies for Sumerian

To make granting permissions easy, IAM supports **managed policies** for each service. A service can update these managed policies with new permissions when it releases new APIs. Sumerian provides managed policies for user permissions needed to use the Sumerian editor.

- `AmazonSumerianFullAccess` – Permission to use all Sumerian features.

```
1  {
2      "Version": "2012-10-17",
3      "Statement": [
4          {
5              "Effect": "Allow",
6              "Action": [
7                  "sumerian:*"
8              ],
9              "Resource": "*"
10         }
11     ]
12 }
```

To add a managed policy to an IAM user, group, or role

1. Open the IAM console.

2. Open the role associated with your instance profile, an IAM user, or an IAM group.

3. Under **Permissions**, attach the managed policy.

You only need access to Sumerians APIs. Sumerian manages all of the storage (Amazon S3) and content delivery (Amazon CloudFront) related to the scenes that you create outside of your account.

Scene Permissions

To use AWS services in a scene, the scene needs credentials as well. You can use Amazon Cognito Identity to create an identity pool that gives the scene access to a role with permission to use AWS. Create a role that has permissions to any services that you will access from scripts, and permissions for components that use AWS services.

To create an identity pool for a Sumerian scene

1. Open the **Federated identities** page in the Amazon Cognito console.

2. Choose **Create new identity pool**.

3. Create a pool with the following settings.

   - **Unauthenticated identities** – enabled

4. Choose **Edit identity pool** to see the pool details.

5. Note the **Identity pool ID** for later use.

When you create an identity pool, Amazon Cognito prompts you to create two roles, an authenticated role, and an unauthenticated role. Add permissions to the unauthenticated role.

To add permissions to an identity pool role for a Sumerian scene

1. Open the **Roles** page in the IAM console.

2. Choose the role named **Cognito_*pool-name*Unauth_Role**.

3. Choose **Attach policy** and add policies for the services that your scene uses.

   - **Speech component** – `AmazonPollyReadOnlyAccess` gives the scene permission to use Amazon Polly to render text into audio with the speech component.
   - **AWS SDK for JavaScript** – add policies that grant access to the services that you call with the SDK for JavaScript. For example, `AmazonS3ReadOnlyAccess`.

Assign the identity pool to your scene under **AWS configuration** in scene settings.

Getting Started with Amazon Sumerian

To get started with Amazon Sumerian, assemble a scene from assets in the Sumerian library. In less than an hour, you can create a scene with effects, animation, and support for virtual reality (VR) headsets. This tutorial also shows basic use of scripting with the speech component, which uses Amazon Polly to render text into audio.

Topics

- Prerequisites
- Create a Project and Scene
- Configure the Scene
- Add and Configure Entities
- Add Behavior
- Add VR Mode
- Publish and View the Scene
- Clean Up
- Next Steps

Prerequisites

To use the Sumerian editor, you need permission to use Sumerian APIs on your IAM user. Additionally, the scene itself needs permission to call Amazon Polly. You provide this permission by creating a role and an Amazon Cognito identity pool. Following the instructions at Amazon Sumerian Permissions to set up both.

You can use the editor in recent versions of Chrome or Firefox. To view the finished scene in VR, use the latest version of Firefox. For VR mode, you also need a compatible headset.

Supported VR Headsets

- Oculus Rift
- Oculus Go
- HTC Vive
- HTC Vive Pro
- Lenovo Mirage Solo

Create a Project and Scene

Create a project and a scene. The project can contain multiple scenes, as well as asset packs and templates that you create from those scenes.

To create a project and scene

1. Open the Sumerian dashboard.

2. Choose **Projects, New project**.

3. Enter **tutorials** for the project name and then choose **Create**.

4. Choose **Create new scene**.

5. Enter **seesaw** for the scene name and then choose **Create**.

Configure the Scene

A skybox is a texture or set of textures that wraps around the scene to provide a background image. Add a skybox from the Sumerian **Asset** library.

To import a skybox from the Sumerian library

1. Choose **Import assets** at the top of the screen.

2. Choose **Blue skysphere**. If you don't find it right away, click the skybox icon to filter the list.

3. Choose **Add**.

This adds the skybox asset pack to the **Asset** panel. The pack contains the skybox asset, and the PNG-formatted texture that the skybox uses. Add the skybox to the scene in the scene settings under **Environment**. While you're there, add some fog and snow.

To configure the scene's environment

1. Choose the root node (**seesaw**) in the **Entities** panel, or click on the background of the scene in the canvas. The groups of options that appear in the inspector panel on the right side of the screen are *scene settings*.

2. Click the **Environment** section to expand it. Expand the **Skybox**, **Fog & Ambient**, and **Particles** sections under it.

3. Click and drag the **Blue skysphere** skybox from the assets panel to the **Drop skybox** field in the inspector panel to attach it to the scene.

4. Choose **Fog** to enable it and configure its parameters:

   - **Fog near** – 5
   - **Fog far** – 20

   This starts fading in fog at 5 units away from the camera, and completely obscures anything 20 units away or farther.

5. Choose **Snow** to enable it, and then configure its parameters:

   - **Velocity** – 20
   - **Rate** – 30
   - **Height** – 100

6. Click the play button at the bottom of the screen to see the snow fall. Adjust the velocity and rate of the snow to your liking. Changes to these settings are applied immediately during playback mode.

Later in this tutorial, you configure the scene to use Amazon Polly to render text into audio during playback. To do this, your scene needs credentials to use the AWS SDK for JavaScript in the web browser. Give the scene credentials by assigning it the ID of the identity pool that you created in the prerequisites section.

To configure AWS SDK for JavaScript credentials

1. Choose the root node in the **Entities** panel.

2. Expand the **AWS configuration** section in the inspector panel.

3. Enter the Amazon Cognito identity pool ID.

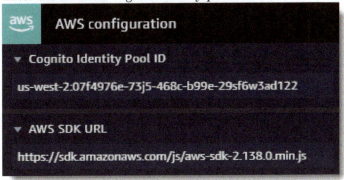

Add and Configure Entities

Add some ground to the scene.

To add a snowy field to your scene

1. Choose **Create entity**.

2. Under **3D primitives**, choose the quad .

   The quad is selected automatically. If you select something else, you can click it in the canvas or entities panel to select it again

3. The quad's components appear in the inspector panel on the right side of the canvas. Expand the top section and change the name of the entity to **ground**. The change is reflected in the section name and entities panel immediately.

4. Expand the **Transform** section, and then enter the following values:

   - **X rotation** – -90
   - **X, Y, and Z scale** – 100
   - **Static** – enabled

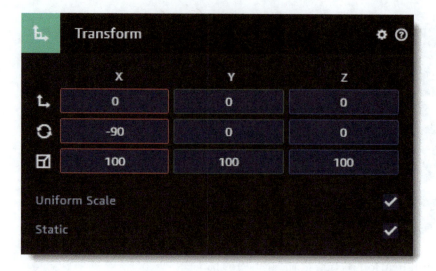

5. Expand the **Material** section and review the settings on each layer. You can click the diffuse or specular colors to choose a different color, or drop image files to add textures.

The space near the camera right now is pretty dark. Add a directional light to light the scene, like the sun is shining in it.

To add a directional light

1. Choose **Create entity**.

2. Under **Lights**, choose **Directional**.

3. Expand the **Transform** section, and then enter the following values:

   - **Y translation** – 10
   - **X rotation** – -30
   - **Y rotation** – -60
   - **Static** – enabled

4. Expand the **Light** section and enable **Shadows**.

Add a blank entity to represent the seesaw, and shapes for the fulcrum and plank.

To add the seesaw

1. Choose **Create entity**.

2. Under **Others**, choose **Entity**.

3. In the inspector panel, change the name of the entity to **seesaw**.

4. Choose **Create entity**, and then add a cylinder to the scene.

5. Rename the cylinder to **fulcrum**, uncheck **Uniform scale**, and set the **Z** scale to **0.6**. Set the diffuse color to yellow.

6. Add a blank entity. Rename it to **plank**. This blank entity will serve as the parent to the plank model, as well as a camera and host entity that will move with the plank.

7. Add a box entity. Rename it to **plank model**. Apply the following transform and set the diffuse color to blue:

   - **Y translation** – .5
   - **Z rotation** – 12
   - **X scale** – 4.5
   - **Y scale** – 0.1

- **Z scale** – 0.6
- **Static** – disabled

Next, import a host from the Sumerian library. Hosts are Sumerian-provided character models with built-in animation and support for speech.

To add a host

1. Choose **Import assets**.

2. Choose **Cristine, Luke,** or **Preston**. Then choose **Add**.

3. When the asset pack finishes loading, drag the host entity from the **Asset** panel to the canvas.

4. Apply the following transform:

- **X translation** – 1.95
- **Y translation** – 0.97
- **Z rotation** – 12
- **Y rotation** – -90
- **X, Y, and Z scale** – 1.3
- **Static** – disabled

Finally, use the **Entities** panel to organize the entities that you created into a hierarchy. Drag an entity onto another one to make them parent and child.

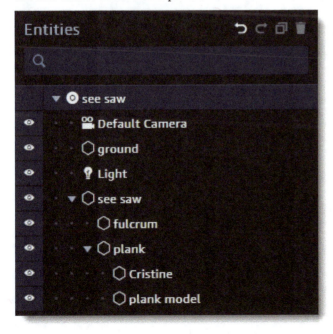

Add Behavior

You can add behavior to your scene by attaching script or state machine components to entities.

A state machine lets you add behavior visually by choosing actions that are triggered by events, and organizing them into states. Add a state machine to the plank entity to animate it and its children.

To animate the plank with a state machine.

1. Choose the **plank** in the entities panel.

2. In the inspector panel, choose **Add component**. Then choose **State machine**.

3. Click the plus symbol next to the behavior field to create a new behavior. Name it **animate**.

4. The **State machine** panel appears with a single state. Name the state **up** , and then choose **Add action**.

5. Under **Animate**, choose **Tween rotate**. Apply the following properties:

   - **Z rotation – -24**
   - **Relative** – disabled
   - **Time – 1000**
   - **Easing type – Linear**
   - **Direction – In**

6. Choose **Add action** again, and then add a **Wait** action. Apply the following properties:

   - **Time – 2000**
   - **Random – 0**

7. In the **State machine** panel, choose **Duplicate state** to make a copy of **up**. Double-click the new state to open it in the inspector panel.

8. Change the state's name to **down**, and then change the rotation value from **-24** to **0**.

9. In the **State machine** panel, each state shows two events, one that occurs at the end of the animation, and one that occurs at the end of the wait action. Click the **On wait end** event under **up** and drag a line to the **down** state. Then do the same in the other direction.

10. Play the scene to watch the seesaw animate.

Add a camera to the other end of the seesaw and make it the default camera. During playback, the user will stay in one location and look around the environment. A built-in camera script allows the user to look around with the mouse prior to entering VR mode.

To add a camera with mouse look controls

1. Choose **Create entity**, and then add a fixed camera to the scene. Rename it to **user**, and then apply the following transform:

   - **X translation – -2.5**
   - **Y translation – 1.2**
   - **Y rotation – -90**

2. In the entities panel, drag the camera onto the **plank** entity to make it move with the seesaw.

3. In the camera's **Camera** component, apply the following properties:

   - **Main camera** – enabled
   - **FOV – 35**

4. Choose **Add component**, and then add a script component to the camera.

5. Click the plus symbol next to the script field, and then choose **Mouse look control**. This adds an instance of the mouse look built-in script. All instances of a script share the same script code, but have separate parameter values.

6. To prevent the user from looking too low, change the **Min ascent** parameter to **-40**.

7. Play the scene and confirm the camera's behavior. Click and drag the left mouse button to look around the scene. You can adjust the script's parameters during playback and see how they affect the controls immediately.

Hosts come with a speech component attached. To use it, you need to add AWS credentials to your scene, add text files to the component, and add a script or state machine component to trigger the speech during playback.

For this example, you'll use a script to do something that the state machine can't—choose and play a file at random. If you haven't already configured AWS credentials for your scene as described in the prerequisites section, do that first.

To configure speech on the host

1. Choose the host in the canvas or entities panel.

2. Under **Speech**, drop some text files onto the speech field. You can use the files in this archive: sonnets.zip.

3. Choose a voice for the host. See Available voices in the *Amazon Polly Developer Guide* for a list of voices sorted by locale.

4. Add a script component to the host.

5. Click the plus symbol next to the script field, and then choose **Custom**.

6. Click edit (pencil icon) in the script instance parameters to open the script in the text editor. You can also press the J key to open the text editor at any time.

7. Double-click the script name (`Script`) in the **Documents** list to change the name to **RandomSpeech**.

8. Replace the placeholder **setup** function with the following.

```
1  var setup = function(args, ctx) {
2    sumerian.SystemBus.addListener('aws.sdkReady',
3      () => {
4        var speechComponent = ctx.entity.getComponent("speechComponent");
5        var speeches = speechComponent.speeches;
6        var speech = speeches[Math.floor(Math.random() * speeches.length)];
7        speech.play();
8      },
9      true
10   );
11 };
```

This script waits for the AWS SDK for JavaScript to load and retrieve credentials. Then it gets a reference to the speech component on the same entity (the host), and gets a list of all of the attached speeches. It chooses a speech from the array and plays it.

9. Play the scene to see the host recite a speech.

10. Return to the speech component and click next to each speech file to add gesture markup.

11. Play the scene again to see the host recite a speech with gestures.

Add VR Mode

So far you've only used a standard camera in playback mode. Add a virtual reality (VR) rig to let users view the scene in 3D with a VR headset and head tracking. Sumerian bundles the entities and scripts required for VR mode in an asset pack named **CoreVR**.

To add VR mode

1. Choose **Import assets**, and then add the **CoreVR** asset pack to your scene.

2. When the asset pack finishes loading, drag the **VRCameraRig** entity onto the canvas to add it to your scene.

3. Choose the **VRCameraRig** entity.

4. Choose the **VRCameraRig** component.

5. Choose the **Current VR camera rig** option to enable the rig.

6. Uncheck the **Start at current camera** option. This enables use of the camera rig where it's placed in the scene, instead of using the location of the non-VR camera when the user enters VR mode.

7. In the entities panel, drag the **VRCameraRig** entity onto the **plank** entity to make it a sibling to the user camera.

8. Choose the **user** camera. Click the cog icon on the **Transform** section, and then choose **Copy** to copy the transform values.

9. Choose the **VRCameraRig**. Click the cog icon on the **Transform** section, and then choose **Paste** to paste the transform values from the user camera.

10. Use the green transform handle to adjust the height of the VR camera relative to the plank.

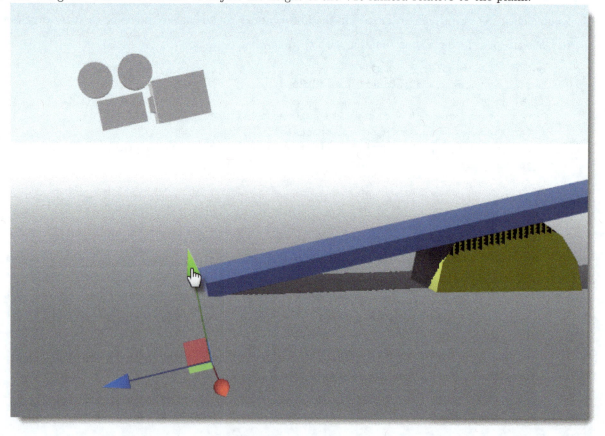

11. Play the scene and click the VR headset icon to enter VR mode.

Publish and View the Scene

Time to share your scene with the world. Publish the scene with Amazon CloudFront to host it as a website that anyone can see.

To publish and view the scene

1. Choose **Publish** from the **Scene** menu in the top left corner of the screen.
2. Choose **Publish**.
3. When the editor finishes publishing the scene, choose **View**.

Clean Up

Your published scene is public and will stay online until you unpublish it.

To unpublish the scene

1. Choose **Publish** from the **Scene** menu in the top left corner of the screen.
2. Choose **Unpublish**.
3. Choose **Yes**.

You can keep the Sumerian scene and project around for use with other tutorials, or delete them. You can always restore the deleted items later from the trash menu.

To delete the project

1. Open the Sumerian dashboard.
2. Choose a project.
3. Under **Project details**, choose **Delete**.

If you created an identity pool for this tutorial and don't plan to use it again, delete it in the Amazon Cognito console.

Next Steps

Learn more about Sumerian in the next chapter, Amazon Sumerian Concepts.

Amazon Sumerian Concepts

Amazon Sumerian lets you create virtual reality (VR) and augmented reality (AR) *scenes* that are made up of *components* and *entities*, organized into *projects*. Let's look closely at the concepts used in the Sumerian editor and this guide.

Scenes

A scene is a 3D space that contains objects and behaviors that define a VR or AR environment. Objects include geometry, materials, and sounds that you import from a supported file format, and objects that you create in the scene like lights, cameras, and particle effects. Behaviors include state machine behaviors, animations, timelines, and scripts.

When you're ready to show off your scene, export it directly to Amazon CloudFront as a static website that you can open in a browser.

See Scenes for more information.

Components and Entities

All objects and behaviors are *components* that combine to create *entities*. For example, when you import a 3D model and add it to a scene, the editor creates an entity that has a geometry component, a material component, a transform component, and an animation component. You can then use the editor to add a rigid body, colliders, and other components to the entity.

See Amazon Sumerian Entities for more information.

Assets

Assets are the images, sounds, scripts, models, and documents that you import into Sumerian to use in a scene. You can manage assets independently of the scenes that use them in the *asset library*. Assets can belong to a user or project.

See Asset Packs for more information.

Hosts

A host is a asset provided by Sumerian that has built in animation, speech, and behavior for interacting with users.

Hosts use Amazon Polly to speak to users from a text source. You can use hosts to engage users and guide them through a VR experience.

See Amazon Sumerian Host Component for more information.

Projects

Projects are an organizational tool for managing scenes, assets, and templates.

See Projects for more information.

Templates

Templates let you save a copy of a scene to use as a starting point for other scenes. Templates belong to a project. Sumerian provides several templates, which you can access from the dashboard.

See Templates for more information.

The Amazon Sumerian Dashboard

The Dashboard is the first thing you see when you open the Amazon Sumerian app. This is where you manage your projects, scenes, asset packs, and templates.

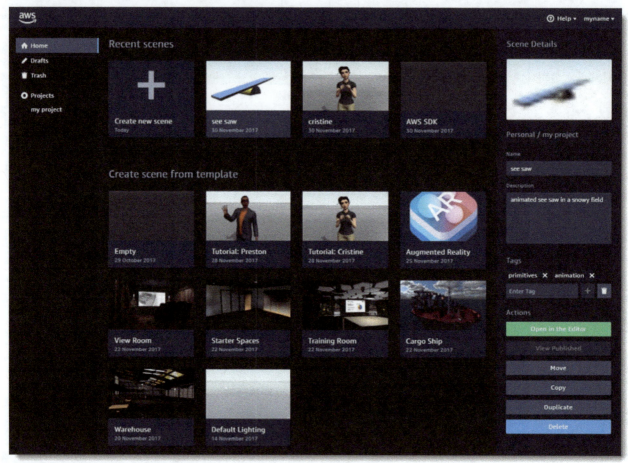

Projects collect scenes and the templates and asset packs that you export from them. You can create draft projects outside of a project, but you must have a project to export templates and assets.

When you open a scene in the editor, it is locked to prevent other users from modifying it. The dashboard manages locks and lets you steal a lock if the other user leaves a scene open by accident.

Topics

- Projects
- Scenes
- Asset Packs
- Templates
- Trash
- Locks

Projects

Projects collect the scenes that you are working on. You can create up to 1,000 projects per region.

To create a project

1. Open the Sumerian dashboard.

2. Choose **Projects**.

3. Choose **New project**.

4. Enter a project name and choose **Create**.

Once you have a project, you can use the dashboard to make a copy or delete it.

To manage a project

1. Open the Sumerian dashboard.

2. Choose a project.

3. Under **Project details**, use one of the following options.

   - **Thumbnail** – Choose **Browse** to upload a thumbnail image.
   - **Name** – Change the project name.
   - **Description** – Change the project description.
   - **Actions** – **Move** or **Copy** the project. **Delete** the project to send it to the **Trash**.
   - **Published URLs** – Choose **View URL List** to get links to all of the project's scenes that have been published in Amazon CloudFront.

Scenes

A scene is a 3D space that you manage in the dashboard and work on in the Sumerian editor. Sumerian provides several templates that you can use as a starting point.

Scenes can be drafts, or part of a project. You can create up to 10,000 scenes per region.

To create a scene

1. Open the Sumerian dashboard.

2. Choose the location to create the scene.

   - **Home** – Create a draft scene.
   - **Drafts** – Create a draft scene.
   - **Project** – Create a scene in one of your projects.

3. Choose **Create scene**.

4. (optional) Choose a template.

5. Enter a scene name and choose **Create**.

When you create a scene, it opens in the Sumerian editor for immediate use. Once you have a scene, you can use the dashboard to make a copy or delete it. Choose the Sumerian icon in the upper left corner to leave the scene and return to the dashboard.

To manage a scene

1. Open the Sumerian dashboard.

2. Locate your scene under **Recent scenes**, **Drafts**, or a project.

3. Choose the scene by clicking its thumbnail. **Note**
   If you click on the name of the scene or double-click the thumbnail, the scene opens in the Sumerian editor.

4. Under **Scene details**, use one of the following options.

   - **Thumbnail** – Choose **Browse** to upload a thumbnail image.
   - **Name** – Change the scene name.
   - **Description** – Change the scene description.
   - **Tags** – Add tags to the scene for use with filters.
   - **Actions**
     - **Open** – Open the scene in the Sumerian editor.
     - **View published** – Open the published version of the scene hosted in Amazon CloudFront.
     - **Move** – Move the scene to a different project.
     - **Copy** – Copy the scene to a different project.
     - **Duplicate** – Create a copy of the scene in the same project.
     - **Delete** – Send the scene to the **Trash**

Additional options for scenes are available in the Sumerian editor scene settings.

Asset Packs

The **Assets** page for a project shows asset packs that have been exported from a scene.

In the dashboard, you can change the name and description of a pack, and copy or move it to another project.

To manage an asset pack

1. Open the Sumerian dashboard.

2. Choose a project.

3. Choose **Assets**.

4. Choose an asset pack.

5. Under **Asset details**, use one of the following options.

   - **Thumbnail** – Choose **Browse** to upload a thumbnail image.
   - **Name** – Change the asset pack name.
   - **Description** – Change the asset pack description.
   - **Tags** – Add tags to the asset pack for use with filters.
   - **Actions**
     - **Move** – Move the asset pack to a different project.
     - **Copy** – Copy the asset pack to a different project.
     - **Delete** – Send the asset pack to the **Trash**

Additional options for asset packs are available in the Sumerian editor.

Templates

Templates are scenes that have been exported from a project for use as a starting point for other scenes. In addition to the templates provided by Sumerian, the dashboard lets you manage templates that you have exported from a scene.

You can use the dashboard to create a scene from a template, or move or copy templates between scenes. Sumerian also provides a library of templates.

To create a scene from a template

1. Open the Sumerian dashboard.

2. Choose **Create new scene**.

3. Choose one of the **Sumerian Templates**, or choose **My templates** to use a template from one of your projects.

4. Enter a name for your scene and choose **Create**.

Create templates from your scenes from the scene settings section in the Sumerian editor. You can then copy your templates to other projects from the **Templates** section of the scene's project page in the dashboard.

To manage a template

1. Open the Sumerian dashboard.

2. Choose a project.

3. Choose **Templates**.

4. Choose a template.

5. Under **Template details**, use one of the following options.

   - **Thumbnail** – Choose **Browse** to upload a thumbnail image.
   - **Name** – Change the template name.
   - **Description** – Change the template description.
   - **Tags** – Add tags to the template for use with filters.
   - **Actions**
     - **Move** – Move the template to a different project.
     - **Copy** – Copy the template to a different project.
     - **Delete** – Send the template to the **Trash**

Trash

When you delete a scene, project, template, or asset pack, Amazon Sumerian moves it to the trash. Items in the trash are retained indefinitely and you can restore them at any time.

You use the trash menu to restore deleted items or delete them permanently.

To restore a deleted item

1. Open the Sumerian dashboard.

2. Choose **Trash**.

3. Choose an item, and then choose **Restore**.

Restored items are returned to their original project.

To avoid paying storage costs for deleted items, delete them permanently.

To delete items permanently

1. Open the Sumerian dashboard.

2. Choose **Trash**.

3. Choose an item, and then choose **Delete**.

   or

   Choose **Empty trash**.

4. Choose **Delete**.

Locks

The Amazon Sumerian editor uses locks to control modifications to a scene. When you open a scene, the editor creates a lock on the scene and refreshes it periodically. If you try to open the scene in a different browser while the lock is active, you will see an error.

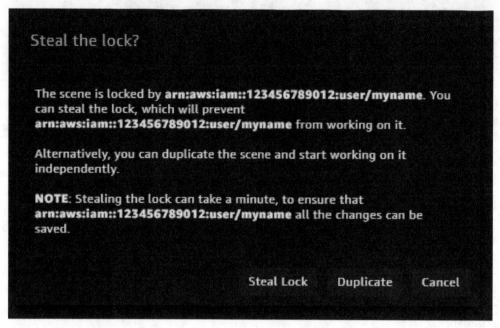

You can force Sumerian to discard the lock if you are sure that no one else is working on the scene, or create a copy of the scene and work on that.

Amazon Sumerian Editor

The Sumerian editor provides an interface for easily importing assets, building a scene, and publishing the scene on the internet.

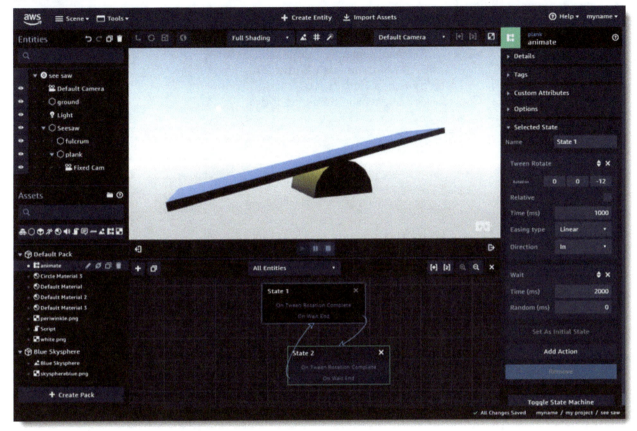

When you load a scene in the Sumerian editor, you can see a menu bar at the top of the screen, the entities panel, the assets panel, the canvas, and the inspector panel. This menu bar provides menus for navigating between scenes, accessing tools, and publishing.

Top bar

- *Sumerian logo*– Exit to dashboard.
- **Scene** – Create a new scene, publish your scene, or open a recent scene.
- **Tools** – Access the text editor, behavior editor, and timeline editor.
- **Create entity** – Add a shape, light, camera, or blank entity to the scene.
- **Import assets** – Open the asset library.
- **Help** – View the shortcut list or submit feedback.
- *Username* – Log out.

The status bar at the bottom of the screen shows updates about save, import, and rendering operations.

Status bar

ℹ finished import	✓ All Changes Saved	myname / Drafts / test

- *Progress bar* – Shows information about the current activity, such as model uploading.

- *Path* – The current user, project, and scene.

The following topics describe the menu options in each of the areas of the editor.

Topics

- Amazon Sumerian Editor Canvas
- Importing Assets From the Asset Library in the Amazon Sumerian Editor
- Using the Assets Panel in the Amazon Sumerian Editor
- Using the Entities Panel in the Amazon Sumerian Editor
- Using the Inspector Panel in the Amazon Sumerian Editor
- Using the Tools in the Amazon Sumerian Editor
- Keyboard and Mouse Controls for the Amazon Sumerian Editor
- Publishing Scenes in the Amazon Sumerian Editor

Amazon Sumerian Editor Canvas

The WebGL-rendered viewport is located in the center of the Sumerian editor. Here you can navigate, inspect, and preview the contents of your scene.

The menu bar at the top of the canvas has options for camera, playback, and rendering. Many of the buttons also have equivalent keyboard commands.

Canvas Menu

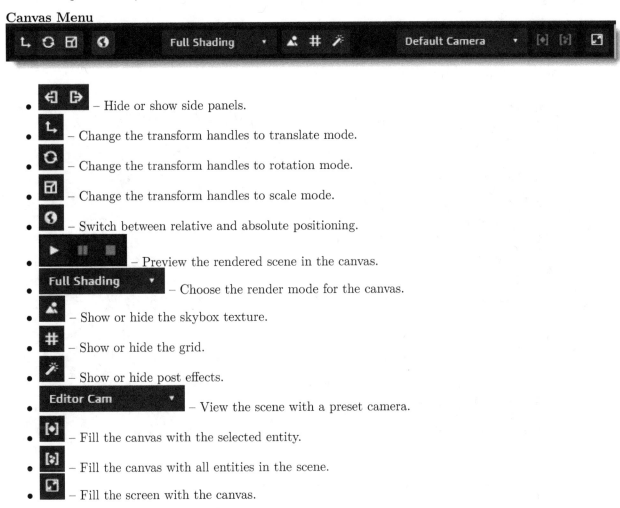

- – Hide or show side panels.
- – Change the transform handles to translate mode.
- – Change the transform handles to rotation mode.
- – Change the transform handles to scale mode.
- – Switch between relative and absolute positioning.
- – Preview the rendered scene in the canvas.
- – Choose the render mode for the canvas.
- – Show or hide the skybox texture.
- – Show or hide the grid.
- – Show or hide post effects.
- – View the scene with a preset camera.
- – Fill the canvas with the selected entity.
- – Fill the canvas with all entities in the scene.
- – Fill the screen with the canvas.

Importing Assets From the Asset Library in the Amazon Sumerian Editor

You can use the Sumerian editor's asset library to import assets from the Sumerian library, your local machine, or from asset packs that you export from a scene.

To import assets

1. Open a scene in the Sumerian editor.

2. Choose **Import assets**.

3. Choose an asset type to filter the available assets by type.

4. Choose an asset pack, and then choose **Add** to add it to your scene's assets.

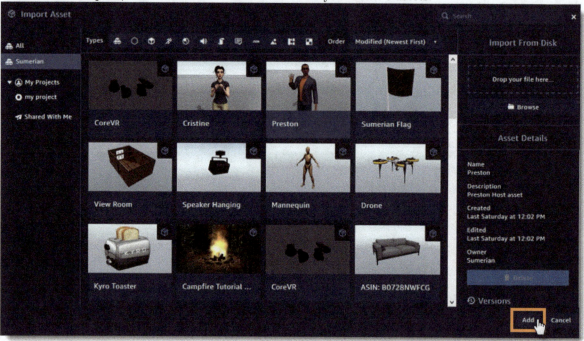

5. After the editor finishes importing the asset pack, drag an entity that it contains from the assets panel onto the canvas to add it to your scene.

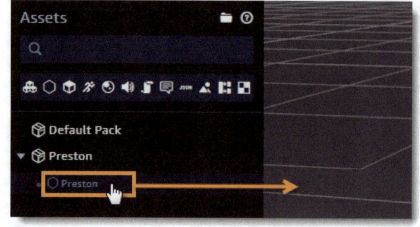

Using the Assets Panel in the Amazon Sumerian Editor

The assets panel shows all assets that belong to the scene. Assets are portable versions of entities or entity components. You can create them from external files or from entities that you create within the editor.

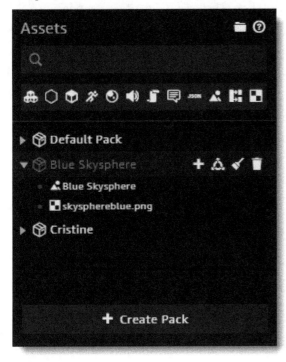

To create an asset, drop a file from your machine, or an entity from the entities panel, onto the assets panel. Depending on the type of file, you may be able to split the file into multiple assets.

For more information, see Amazon Sumerian Assets.

Using the Entities Panel in the Amazon Sumerian Editor

The entities panel shows you a scene's entities in a hierarchy, starting with the scene itself. An entity can be a child of the scene or of another entity. When you choose the scene in the entities panel, the inspector panel shows the scene's settings. When you choose an entity, the inspector panel shows the entity's components.

Organize your entities by their physical or logical relationship to other entities. An entity's position, rotation, and scale are relative to its parent. When you move the parent, the child moves as well. To change an entity's parent, drag it onto the new parent in the entities panel.

Entities panel controls

- ▼ – Collapse the entity to hide its children in the entities panel.
- 👁 – Hide or show an entity in the canvas.
- 🗐 – Duplicate an entity.
- 🗑 – Delete an entity.
- ↺ ↻ – Undo or redo changes.

Using the Inspector Panel in the Amazon Sumerian Editor

Use the inspector panel to manage scene settings, entities, and assets. When you select any of these elements in the Sumerian editor, you get the following properties in a section named after the element.

Generic properties

- **Thumbnail** – The thumbnail image for the element. Drop an image onto the thumbnail field or pause your mouse over it. Then choose **Take screenshot** to save an image of the current view of the canvas.
- **Name** – The name of the element.
- **ID** (read-only) – A unique identifier for the element.
- **Type** (read-only) – The type of element: scene, entity, or an asset type.
- **Description** – Description of the element.
- **Tags** – Key-only metadata that you can use in scripting. You can read tags or search for entities with specific tags by using the context object.
- **Custom attributes** – Key-value metadata that you can use in scripting. You can read attributes by using the context object.

When you choose the scene in the entities panel, or click the scene's background in the canvas, the inspector panel shows several additional sections for settings that apply to the entire scene. These include environmental settings, post-processing effects, and AWS SDK credentials. See Amazon Sumerian Scene Settings for more information.

When you choose an entity in the entities panel, or click it in the canvas, the inspector panel shows a section for each component on the entity. At a minimum, every entity has a transform component that determines its location, rotation, and size. Entities you create by dropping assets onto the scene have additional components based on their type. You can add components to any entity in the inspector panel by choosing **Add component** at the bottom of the panel. See Amazon Sumerian Entities for more information.

When you choose an asset in the assets panel, the inspector panel shows sections for only components that apply to every instance of the asset in the scene. For example, a script asset only has code, but a script component on an entity can have parameters that customize that instance of the script. A material asset, however, has all of the material component properties. Modifying any of these properties changes every instance of the material in the scene.

Using the Tools in the Amazon Sumerian Editor

The Sumerian editor has three tool panels for working with complex assets and components:

- The **text** editor provides an interface for authoring scripts, JSON documents, and speech files.
- The **timeline** editor animates entities between keyframes.
- The **state machine** editor lets you visually construct and connect state machine behaviors and actions.

Text Editor

The text editor lets you view and modify all text assets in the scene, including scripts, JSON documents, and speech files.

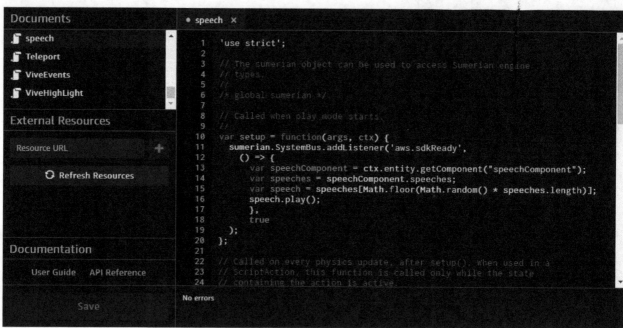

To use the text editor, choose **Tools, Text editor**. Or press the J key.

The **Documents** panel lists the text assets in your scene. Click one to open it in a tab. To rename an asset, highlight it and click the pencil icon.

When you open a script, the **External Resources** panel appears. You can use this panel to import librariesfrom the internet that your script depends on. See External Dependencies for more information.

State Machine Editor

The state machine editor provides a visual representation of the actions and behaviors attached to a state machine component.

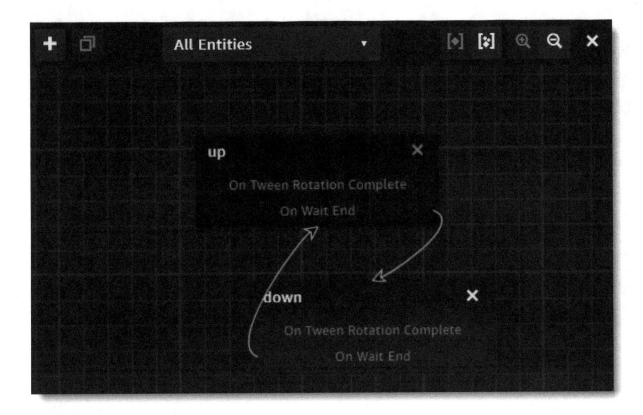

To use the state machine editor, click the pencil icon next to a behavior in the assets panel or on a state machine component.

The state machine editor shows a box for each behavior. Each box has a stack of actions, listed in the order that they execute. When an action transitions to another behavior, an arrow connects the action to the target behavior. Click an action and drag the cursor to a behavior to create a transition between the two.

For more information, see Amazon Sumerian State Machines.

Timeline

Use timelines to move, rotate, or change the scale of entities over time. You can set the start and end values of these properties, and add keyframes to control the speed or direction of the animation along the way. The timeline can also emit custom events, which can be consumed from a state machine or script.

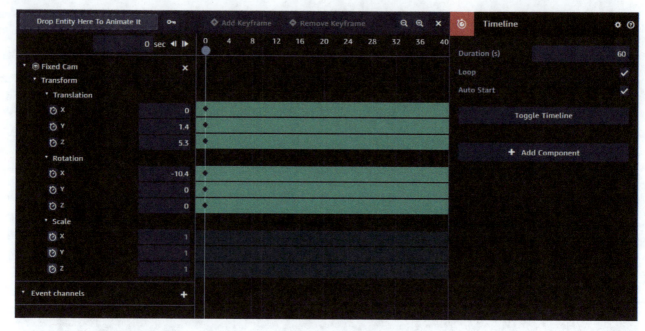

For more information, see Amazon Sumerian Timeline Component.

Keyboard and Mouse Controls for the Amazon Sumerian Editor

The default camera that Sumerian adds to every scene supports mouse controls for pan, zoom, and orbiting around the camera's anchor point. To move the camera, press and hold a mouse button while you move the mouse. If you only have one mouse button, you can use a keyboard key plus mouse button combination to perform the same movements.

Camera Movement

- **Zoom in or out** – Mouse wheel scroll up or down
- **Pan** – Mouse wheel button, or ShiftLeft mouse button
- **Orbit** – Right mouse button, or AltLeft mouse button

The Sumerian editor provides keyboard equivalents of most of the canvas menu buttons. Use the bottom row of keys to switch between preset camera views, and the F key to fill the canvas with a single entity. The space bar hides the side panels to let the canvas fill the screen.

Camera

- **Frame entity** – F
- **Frame all** – ShiftF
- **Bottom and top views** – V
- **Back and front views** – C
- **Left and right views** – X
- **Editor camera view** – Z
- **Show and hide side bars** – Space

Select entities by clicking them in either the editor or the **Entities** panel. With an entity selected, use the following commands to speed up editing.

Editing

- **Delete entity** – Backspace or Delete
- **Duplicate entity** – Ctrl D
- **Translate handles** – W
- **Rotation handles** – E
- **Scale handles** – R
- **Switch between global and relative transform** – G
- **Undo** – Ctrl Z
- **Redo** – Ctrl Shift Z

Use the following commands to open the text editor, timeline editor, and publishing menu.

Tools

- **Text editor** – J
- **Timeline** – T
- **Publish** – Ctrl Shift P

With the timeline open, use the following commands to adjust keyframes and playheads.

Timeline

- **Move keyframe left** – Left (fast), Ctrl Left (slow)
- **Move keyframe right** – Right (fast), Ctrl Right (slow)
- **Move playhead left** – Shift Left (fast), Ctrl Shift Left (slow)
- **Move playhead right** – Shift Right (fast), Ctrl Shift Right (slow)
- **Align keyframe left** – Ctrl Alt 1
- **Align keyframe center** – Ctrl Alt 2
- **Align keyframe right** – Ctrl Alt 3
- **Move keyframe to start** – Home

- **Move keyframe to end** – End

Publishing Scenes in the Amazon Sumerian Editor

Publish your Sumerian scene to share it with users on the internet. When you publish a scene, Sumerian creats a static website with your scene and hosts it on Amazon CloudFront. You can link users directly to the scene, or embed it in a frame in your website.

To publish a scene

1. Open your scene in the Sumerian editor.

2. Choose **Scene**, and then choose **Publish**.

3. Configure publishing settings.

   - **Custom CSS** – Specify the contents of a `style` tag to add to the generated webpage.
   - **Custom JavaScript** – Specify the contents of a `script` tag to add to the generated webpage.

4. Choose **Publish**.

After a few seconds, your scene is live. You can click **View** to open it.

Amazon Sumerian Scene Settings

In addition to the options available in the dashboard, the Sumerian editor contains many options for configuring a scene. In the inspector panel, you can configure credentials for the AWS SDK for JavaScript, adjust the canvas size and grid, and configure global settings like fog, background image, and post-processing effects.

To configure a scene

1. Open a scene in the Sumerian editor.

2. Choose the root node in the **Entities** panel.

3. Modify scene settings in the inspector panel.

   - **Details** – Update the scene's name and description.
   - **Tags** – Add metadata tags to the scene.
   - **Custom attributes** – Add metadata key-value pairs to the scene.

You can save a copy of your scene as a **template** to use as a starting point for creating other scenes. If your scene is saved to a project, the template is saved to the same project. Otherwise, you must choose a project to hold the template.

To create a template

1. Open a scene in the Sumerian editor.

2. Choose the root node in the **Entities** panel.

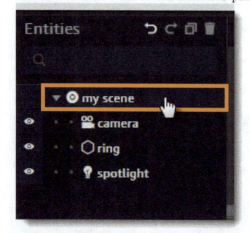

3. Expand the scene section in the inspector panel.

4. Choose **Save scene as template**.

5. If the scene is a draft, choose a project for the template.

You can copy or move templates between scenes in the dashboard. You can update a template by creating a template again from the same source scene or from a scene created from the template. When you save a template, you can choose to create a new template or update the existing template.

Collapse the scene settings section by choosing the name of your scene.

Topics

- Configuring AWS Credentials for Your Amazon Sumerian Scene
- Creating Snapshots of Your Amazon Sumerian Scene
- Configuring the Canvas for Your Amazon Sumerian Scene
- Configuring Environment Settings for Your Amazon Sumerian Scene
- Configuring Post-Processing Effects for Your Amazon Sumerian Scene
- Calculating the Size of Your Amazon Sumerian Scene
- Viewing Performance Information for Your Amazon Sumerian Scene

Configuring AWS Credentials for Your Amazon Sumerian Scene

The **AWS configuration** section lets you configure credentials to use with the AWS SDK for JavaScript. You can set a Amazon Cognito identity pool ID, which Sumerian uses to retrieve credentials when the scene is loaded. The identity pool must have an unauthenticated role with permission to use the AWS APIs that your scripts access.

Note
If you don't have an identity pool, follow the instructions under Amazon Sumerian Permissions to create one.

To configure AWS SDK for JavaScript credentials

1. Open a scene in the Sumerian editor.

2. Choose the root node in the **Entities** panel.

3. Expand the **AWS configuration** section in the inspector panel.

4. Enter an Amazon Cognito identity pool ID.

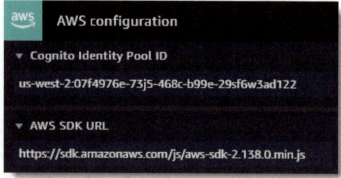

To use the credentials, create a script that listens for `aws.sdkReady` before initializing an SDK for JavaScript client. The following example lists the contents of an Amazon S3 bucket named `mybucket` in the browser console. To test its functionality, create a script, attach it to an entity, and play the scene.

Example S3listobjects script

```
1  'use strict';
2
3  var setup = function(args, ctx) {
4      sumerian.SystemBus.addListener('aws.sdkReady',
5          () => {
6              let s3 = new AWS.S3();
```

```
 7          s3.listObjects({Bucket: "mybucket"}, function(err, data) {
 8              if (err) {
 9                  console.log('ERROR', err, data);
10              } else {
11                  console.log('DATA', data);
12              }
13          }
14        );
15      },
16      true
17    );
18 };
```

Creating Snapshots of Your Amazon Sumerian Scene

You can use the Snapshots panel to create a copy of your scene that you can use to restore your scene later. Create snapshots to set a restore point prior to trying new features or making sweeping changes to your scene.

To create a snapshot

1. Open a scene in the Sumerian editor.

2. Choose the root node in the **Entities** panel.

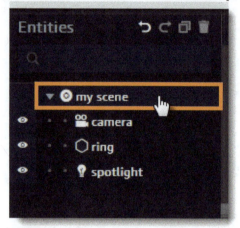

3. Expand the **Snapshots** section in the inspector panel.

4. Enter a description.

5. Choose **Create**.

To restore or delete a snapshot

1. Open a scene in the Sumerian editor.

2. Choose the root node in the **Entities** panel.

3. Expand the **Snapshots** section in the inspector panel.

4. Choose a snapshot.

5. Choose **Restore** or **Delete**.

47

Configuring the Canvas for Your Amazon Sumerian Scene

You can use the document panel to configure the size of the WebGL canvas and grid color. These settings apply only while you are working on a scene in the editor, and to the published scene.

To configure the canvas using document settings

1. Open a scene in the Sumerian editor.

2. Choose the root node in the **Entities** panel.

3. Expand the **Document** section in the inspector panel.

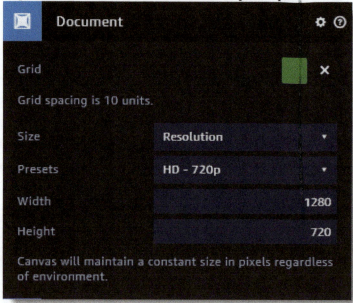

4. Choose from the following options:

   - **Grid** – Change the color of the grid.
   - **Stretch** – Stretch the canvas to its container.
   - **Aspect ratio** – Stretch the canvas to its container, but keep the aspect ratio.
   - **Resolution** – Set a fixed size of the canvas.

Configuring Environment Settings for Your Amazon Sumerian Scene

Use environment settings to configure your scene's background image, ambient lighting, and weather.

To configure environment settings

1. Open a scene in the Sumerian editor.

2. Choose the root node in the **Entities** panel.

3. Expand the **Environment** section in the inspector panel.

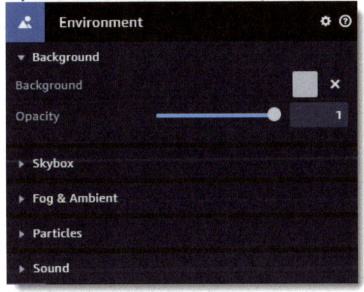

4. Configure the following settings:

   - **Background** – Set the background color of the scene, and its opacity.

     To make the background transparent, set **Opacity** to 0. If you add a skybox, background settings have no effect.

   - **Skybox** – Use an image as the background of the scene. You can drop an existing skybox from the assets panel, or choose the plus icon to create a new skybox.

   - **Ambient** – Add ambient light to light all objects in the scene. Ambient light doesn't affect the skybox.

- **Fog** – Add fog to the scene. Fog starts occluding objects in the scene at **Fog near** units from the camera, and strengthens until **Fog far** units, where the fog becomes completely opaque.

- **Particles** – Add animated snow-like particles to the background of the scene.

Properties + **Velocity** – The speed of the falling particles. + **Rate** – The number of particles that appear per second. + **Height** – The height at which the particles will appear, relative to the camera height.

Configuring Post-Processing Effects for Your Amazon Sumerian Scene

In the post effects section of the inspector panel, you can add rendering effects like antialiasing and motion blur. Post effects are not compatible with VR mode.

To add post effects

1. Open a scene in the Sumerian editor.

2. Choose the root node in the **Entities** panel.

3. Expand the **Post effects** section in the inspector panel.

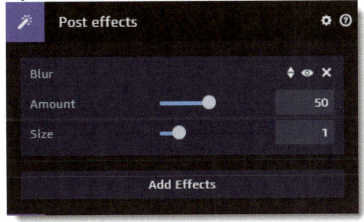

4. Choose **Add effects**.

5. Choose one or more effects, and then choose **Add**.

6. Adjust the settings for each effect in the inspector panel.

7. See how post effects affect rendering by clicking the post effects icon ![icon] in the canvas toolbar to toggle them on and off.

Post effects properties

- **Antialias** – Add FXAA-based antialiasing to smooth out jagged edges.
  - **Span** – The area of the smoothing effect.
- **Bloom** – Make bright background colors bleed over the edges of foreground objects.

- **Opacity** – The amount of bloom applied.
- **Size** – The size of the glow area.
- **Gain** – The amount of brightness added.
- **Intensity** – The amount of contrast.
- **Bleach** – Alter input color by its luminance.
  - **Opacity** – The blending multiplier for the effect.
- **Blur** – Blur the entire scene to make it appear out of focus.
  - **Amount** – The amount of blending that causes the blur.
  - **Size** –The size of the blur area.
- **Contrast** – Adjust the brightness, contrast, and saturation.
  - **Brightness** – Remove or add brightness.
  - **Contrast** – Adjust the contrast.
  - **Saturation** – Adjust the color saturation.
- **Dot** – Add a black-and-white lattice effect.
  - **Angle** – The angle of the lattice.
  - **Scale** – The thickness of the lattice.
  - **SizeX** – Skew the lattice on the X axis.
  - **SizeY** – Skew the lattice on the Y axis.
- **Edge detect** – Add a *difference of Gaussians*-based edge detection.
  - **Gauss Sigma** – The base of the two Gaussian kernels.
  - **Threshold** – The edge detection tolerance value.
  - **Background %** – The amount of blending between the background and edge colors.
  - **Edge Color** – The edge color.
  - **Background Color** – The background color.
- **Film grain** – Add noise and resolution lines.
  - **Noise** – The amount of noise.
  - **Line Intensity** – The sharpness of the lines.
  - **Line Count** – The number of lines.
- **Hatch** – Render the scene in black and white, with a lattice effect over black areas.
  - **Width** – The width of the lattice lines.
  - **Spread** – The distance between the lattice lines.
- **HSB** (hue, saturation, and brightness) – Adjust colors of the scene.
  - **Hue** – Adjust the hue.
  - **Saturation** – Adjust the color saturation.
  - **Brightness** – Adjust the image brightness.
- **Levels** – Apply gamma correction to the image.
  - **Gamma** – Adjust the gamma level.
  - **Min input** and **Max input** – The gamma input range.
  - **Min output** and **Max output** – The gamma output range.
- **Motion Blur** – Apply a blur effect to objects that moved since the previous rendered frame. If the camera moves, the entire image blurs.
  - **Amount** – The amount of blending.
  - **Scale** – Overlay the previous frame on top of the current frame at a different scale to create a zooming or flying effect.
- **Noise** – Add signal noise to the image.
  - **Noise** – The amount of signal noise.
- **Overlay** – Overlay a texture on the image.
  - **Texture** – The texture asset.
  - **Blend mode** – The method of blending the overlay and background.
  - **Amount** – The amount of blending.
- **Radial** – Add a radial blur to the image.
  - **Offset** – The blur offset.
  - **Multiplier** – The blur multiplier.
- **RGB shift** – Split the image into red, green, and blue layers with an offset between layers.

- **Amount** – The distance between the layers.
  - **Angle** – The angle in radians between the layers.
- **Sepia** – Add a sepia color filter.
  - **Amount** – The intensity of the effect.
- **Tint** – Apply a color filter to the image.
  - **Color** – The tint color.
  - **Amount** – The intensity of the effect.
- **Vignette** – Add a dark gradient around the edges of the image.
  - **Offset** – The size of the gradient.
  - **Darkness** – The strength of the gradient.

Calculating the Size of Your Amazon Sumerian Scene

The **Scene Size** section calculates how much data your scene is using. You can see the number of kilobytes from JSON, mesh data, and binaries.

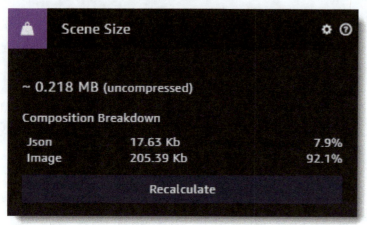

The numbers shown reflect the uncompressed size of the scene. When a scene is served from Amazon CloudFront, the contents are compressed. To see the compressed size, open your scene and use the network tab of the browser developer tools to find the amount of data transferred.

Viewing Performance Information for Your Amazon Sumerian Scene

The **Scene stats** section gives you some performance statistics about the current scene.

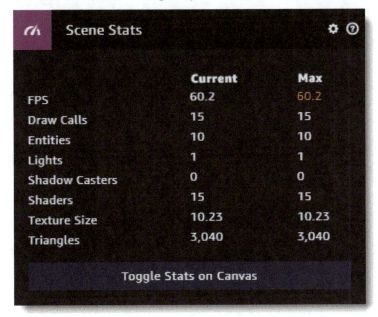

Stats

- **FPS** – The number of frames rendered per second.
- **Draw calls** – The number of draw calls made per frame.
- **Entities** – The number of visible entities.
- **Lights** – The number of lights being rendered.
- **Shadow casters** – The number of shadow casters being rendered.
- **Shaders** – The number of shaders being rendered.
- **Texture size** – The current texture size in the GPU.
- **Triangles** – The number of triangles being rendered.

To improve performance, try reducing the number of draw calls, lights, and shaders.

Amazon Sumerian Entities

Entities are a kind of container in Sumerian that you use to collect and organize assets in your scene. For example, when you add a 3D model to your scene, the editor splits it into mesh, texture, and animation assets and assigns them to an entity with the corresponding Sumerian geometry, material, and animation components. Your scene can contain up to 1,000 entities.

Entities can be cameras, lights, or containers for other entities. The Entities panel organizes entities into a hierarchy. You can use it to attach entities to one another in parent-child relationships.

Components are the configurable parts of an entity that determine its appearance and behavior during playback. To make a lamp model light the scene, add a light component. To move or change the entity during playback, add a state machine, timeline, or script component.

To create an entity and add components

1. Open a scene in the Sumerian editor.

2. Choose **Create entity**.

3. Choose a shape or built-in object. For a blank entity, choose **Entity**.

4. Choose the new entity in the entities panel.

5. In the inspector panel, expand the **Details** section. Enter text in the fields to change the entity name, description, tags, and attributes.

6. To place the entity in the scene, use the X, Y, and Z axis handles in the canvas. Or expand the **Transform** section and enter absolute coordinates.

7. Choose the plus icon, and then choose a component type to add a component to the entity.

Managing Entities

Use the entities panel to organize your scene's entities in a hierarchy. When you make an entity a child of another entity, it attaches to the parent. That is, when you move the parent, the child moves, and when you set the child's position, it's relative to the position of the parent.

To manage entities

1. Open a scene in the Sumerian editor.

2. Choose an entity in the entities panel.

3. Drag the entity onto another entity to make it a child of that entity.

4. Use the icons next to the entity name to manage it the eye icon next to an entity to hide it.

- – Hide the entity.

- – Make a copy of the entity.

- – Delete the entity.

Managing Components

Components have properties you can use to configure settings or attach assets. All entities include a transform component that you can use to move the entity around the scene. Depending on the type of entity that you create, other components are also included automatically.

Default Components

- **2D shapes** – Transform, 2d graphics
- **3D shapes** – Transform, geometry, material
- **Cameras** – Transform, camera, script
- **HTML 3D** – Transform, HTML 3D
- **Lights** – Transform, light
- **Particles** – Transform, particles
- **Timeline** – Transform, timeline

To manage components

1. Open a scene in the Sumerian editor.

2. Choose an entity in the entities panel.

3. In the inspector panel, choose a component's name to expand or collapse its properties. See the topics below for each component for details on their available properties.

4. Click the cog icon and use the following options:

   - **Reset** – Restore the default values for the component's properties.
   - **Toggle panel** – Show or hide the component properties.
   - **Remove** – Delete the component.
   - **Copy** (some components) – Copy the component configuration.
   - **Paste** (some components) – Paste the component configuration that you copied from the same component on a different entity.

Some components also have special properties that are affected by the components on their parent. For example, a collider's behavior changes depending on the type of rigid body that's attached to the same entity or parent entity.

The following topics describe the parameters and use of each type of component.

Basic Components

- Amazon Sumerian Transform Component
- Amazon Sumerian Geometry Component
- Amazon Sumerian Material Component
- Amazon Sumerian Camera Component
- Amazon Sumerian VR Camera Rig Component
- Amazon Sumerian HMD Camera Component
- Amazon Sumerian VR Controller Component
- Amazon Sumerian Host Component
- Amazon Sumerian Speech Component

- Amazon Sumerian Dialogue Component

Content and Effects

- Amazon Sumerian 2D Graphics Component
- Amazon Sumerian HTML Components
- Amazon Sumerian Sound Component
- Amazon Sumerian Light Component
- Amazon Sumerian Particle System Component

Animation and Physics

- Amazon Sumerian Animation Component
- Amazon Sumerian Collider Component
- Amazon Sumerian Rigid Body Component
- Amazon Sumerian State Machine Component
- Amazon Sumerian Script Component
- Amazon Sumerian Timeline Component

Amazon Sumerian Transform Component

The transform component contains the local transform of the component –translation, rotation, and scale. The transform is relative to its parent.

Properties

- **Translation** – Position of the object relative to its parent.
- **Rotation** – Rotation of the object in degrees.
- **Scale** – Size of the object.
- **Uniform scale** – Proportions to maintain when scale is modified on any axis.
- **Static** – Optimization of the object's rendering based on it not moving during playback.

Amazon Sumerian Geometry Component

The geometry component contains a renderable mesh or primitive on the entity. When you import a 3D model, or create a primitive from the **Create entity** menu, it always gets a geometry component.

Together with a material component, you can render the entity. If you don't have a material component, the geometry is invisible.

The panel looks different for different kinds of meshes and primitives, but in general, they have these settings:

Properties

- Cast shadows
- Receive shadows
- Dimensions and/or number of samples (primitives only)

Amazon Sumerian Material Component

When you add a 3D model to your environment, it has at least two components. The geometry component defines the shape of the model. The material component defines its textures and rendering properties.

Properties

- **Diffuse color** – The base color of the surface.

  - **Color** – The base diffuse color.
  - **Texture** – The diffuse color from a texture.

- **Normal** – A type of bump map. Normal maps are a special kind of texture that you use to add surface detail such as bumps, grooves, and scratches to a model. These details catch the light as if they are represented by real geometry.

  You set the normal map via the **Texture** input, and you can alter its magnitude by setting the **Strength** value.

- **Specular** – Specular effects, which are essentially the direct reflections of light sources in your scene. These typically show up as bright highlights or shininess on the surface of objects (although specular highlights can be subtle or diffuse, too).

  You can set the base specularity **Color**, use a **Texture**, and set the **shininess** value.

- **Emissive** – The self-illumination color of an object. You can set the emissive color by using the **Color** input and/or by using a **Texture**.

- **Ambient** – The color of an object where it is in shadow. This color is what the object reflects when illuminated by ambient light instead of direct light.

  - **Color** The base ambient color.
  - **Texture** Ambient map that identifies areas on a mesh that are exposed or hidden from ambient lighting.

- **Opacity** – Used with transparency blending. You can use **Strength** to input a value between 0 and 1, where 0.0 represents completely transparent and 1.0 represents fully opaque.

  - **Threshold** – Used to indicate when a surface is completely transparent, and can be discarded from rendering.
  - **Dual transparency** – Render both front and back surfaces of the material.

- **Reflectivity** – Reflectivity settings for the material.

  - **Texture** – Reflectivity texture.
  - **Environment** – Environment map that you see in the reflection. If not selected, the current skybox is used.
  - **Amount** – Amount of reflectivity to use.
  - **Fresnel** – A nonzero fresnel value results in less reflection, depending on the normal direction.

- **Refractivity** – Refraction input. Takes in a texture or value that simulates the surface's index of refraction. This is useful for things like glass and water, which refract light that passes through them. The environment texture is used for the refraction.

  - **Amount** – How much refraction to blend with the current color.
  - **Refraction** – Ratio of the refractive indices involved in the refraction.

- **Blending** – Blending mode to use for the material.

  - **NoBlending**
  - **TransparencyBlending**
  - **CustomBlending**
  - **AdditiveBlending**

- SubtractiveBlending
- MultiplyBlending

- **Culling** – Whether to cull on the triangle level, and which face (back, front, both) to cull.

- **Depth** – Whether to enable depth testing or depth writing, and which **RenderQueue** value to use.

- **Shading**

    - **Flat** – Turn on flat shading for the mesh.
    - **Wireframe** – Render the mesh in wireframe mode.
    - **Wrap factor** – The light wrap factor.
    - **Wrap amount** – The light wrap amount.

Note

You can share material assets between entities. If a material asset is shared, changing the look of one entity also changes the ones that are sharing the material.

Amazon Sumerian Camera Component

The camera component adds a camera to your entity. In the Amazon Sumerian editor, you can use it to define your 3D viewport.

Properties

- **Main camera** – Use this camera at the beginning of the scene. If you have multiple cameras, you can switch between them during both edit and playback modes.
- **Follow editor camera** – Set the camera position with the editor camera. This is useful when switching between edit and play modes.
- **Projection** – Control how the camera will project the 3D world on the 2D canvas.
- **Field of view (FOV)** – Set the number of degrees from left to right that the camera will span.
- **Clipping planes** – Set the distance from the camera at which objects are drawn.

Amazon Sumerian VR Camera Rig Component

The VR camera rig component configures a virtual reality (VR) headset and controllers for use in VR mode during playback. When a user has a supported headset, they can click the VR button to switch between the main camera and the head mounted display (HMD) camera that represents a VR headset.

Supported VR Headsets

- Oculus Rift
- Oculus Go
- HTC Vive
- HTC Vive Pro
- Lenovo Mirage Solo

Attach the VR camera rig component to an entity with child entities for the HMD camera and each VR controller. The CoreVR asset pack in the Sumerian library contains a rig entity with an HMD camera and controllers for each supported headset.

Properties

- **Load gamepads** – Deselect to disable controllers.
- **Start at current camera** – Deselect to use the camera from its transform location, instead of swapping out the main camera for the VR rig when the user enters VR mode.
- **Current VR camera rig** – Select to use this rig in VR mode.

Amazon Sumerian HMD Camera Component

The HMD camera component represents a head mounted display (HMD) in a VR camera rig. When you attach an entity with an HMD camera component to a VR camera rig, users can use a VR headset to view the scene in VR mode.

This component doesn't have any configurable properties. See Amazon Sumerian VR Camera Rig Component for more information.

Amazon Sumerian VR Controller Component

The VR controller component represents a single virtual reality (VR) controller in a VR camera rig. When a user enters VR mode with a controller attached, the VR controller component tracks its location in 3D space.

See Amazon Sumerian VR Camera Rig Component for more information.

Properties

- **ID** – Controller type that this entity represents.

Amazon Sumerian Host Component

A host is an asset provided by Sumerian that has built in animation, speech, and behavior for interacting with users. Add a host to your scene from the asset library.

When you add a host to your scene, it includes a **Host** component for configuring the host's behavior, and a **speech** component that you can use to configure the host's voice and script.

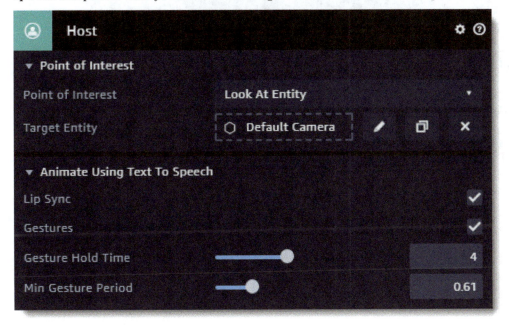

Properties

- **Point of interest** – Set to **Look at entity** to keep the host's eyes trained on a camera, object, or other entity during playback.
- **Target entity** – Drop an entity here to set it as the host's point of interest.
- **Lip sync** – Play lip sync animations during speech.
- **Gestures** – Play gesture animations during speech.
- **Gesture hold time** – Set the number of seconds to play a gesture animation.
- **Minimum gesture period** – Set the number of seconds to wait after a gesture is complete before another gesture can occur.

Amazon Sumerian Speech Component

The speech component assigns text to an entity for playback with Amazon Polly. You assign text to an entity, and play the audio output from Amazon Polly with a state machine or script. The scene calls Amazon Polly at runtime to generate the audio.

To use Amazon Polly during playback, the scene needs AWS credentials from Amazon Cognito Identity. Create an identity pool for your scene, and configure it under AWS configuration in the scene settings.

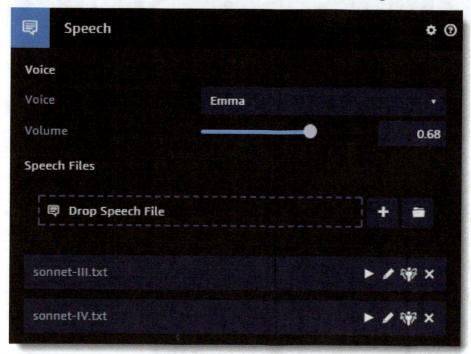

Properties

- **Voice** – An Amazon Polly voice.
- **Volume** – Volume of the rendered audio.
- **Speech files** – Drop text files here to add them to the component. Click to mark up a speech file with gestures.

To trigger a speech during playback, use a state machine or script component on the same entity.

State Machine

To play a speech, add a state machine to the entity with the speech component. Add a state with **AWS SDK ready** and **Start speech** actions.

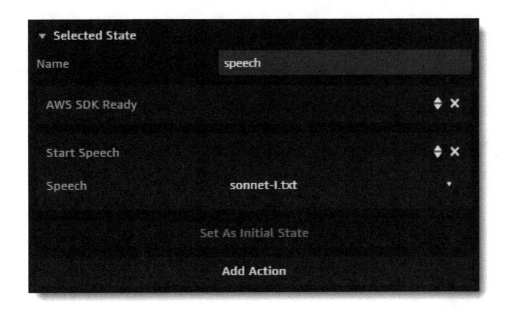

Script

To play a speech, get a reference to the speech component from the context object. The component has a `speeches` array that contains the speeches attached to the component. Call `play` on a speech.

Sumerian calls Amazon Polly when you play a speech, so you must use the `aws.sdkReady` listener to ensure that your scene's AWS credentials are loaded before the call.

Example script – play a random speech

```
1 'use strict';
2 var setup = function(args, ctx) {
3 sumerian.SystemBus.addListener('aws.sdkReady',
4   () => {
5     var speechComponent = ctx.entity.getComponent("speechComponent");
6     var speeches = speechComponent.speeches;
7     var speech = speeches[Math.floor(Math.random() * speeches.length)];
8     speech.play();
9   },
10   true
11 );
12 };
```

Amazon Sumerian Dialogue Component

The dialogue component assigns an Amazon Lex chatbot to an entity. You can use this component to enable a host or other entity to converse with a user and collect information.

To use Amazon Lex during playback, the scene needs AWS credentials from Amazon Cognito Identity. Create an identity pool for your scene, and configure it under AWS configuration in the scene settings.

Properties

- **Name** – The name of the Amazon Lex bot.
- **Alias** – The alias that you choose when you publish the bot.

To trigger dialogue during playback, use a state machine or script component on the same entity.

State Machine

To use an Amazon Lex bot, add a state machine to an entity with dialogue and speech components. Use actions to capture audio or text, send it to Amazon Lex for processing, play the response, and wait for additional input.

Example States for text input

- **Initialize – AWS SDK ready** waits for the AWS SDK for JavaScript to retrieve credentials from your Amazon Cognito identity pool.

- **Collect text** – A **Get HTML text** action that retrieves the contents of the `input` element in an HTML component.

  - **Entity** – An HTML element with an `input` element.
  - **HTML element selector** – The ID of the `input` element. For example, **#myTagId**.

- **Send to bot – Send text input to dialogue bot** sends the text from the previous state to your Amazon Lex bot and relays the response to the next state.

  Transition **On response ready** to `Play response`, and **On processing error** to `Collect text`.

- **Play response – Start speech** plays the response from Amazon Lex. Transition to `Collect text`.

  - **Use Lex response** – Enabled.

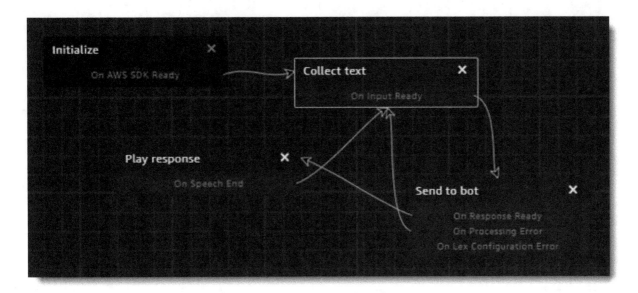

Example States for audio input

- **Initialize – AWS SDK ready** waits for the AWS SDK for JavaScript to retrieve credentials from your Amazon Cognito identity pool.
- **Record (1) – Key down** waits for the user to press a key.
- **Record (2) – Start microphone recording** records audio and **Key up** waits for the user to release the key.
- **Record (3) – Stop microphone recording** completes the audio recording and passes it to the next state.
- **Send to bot – Send audio input to dialogue bot** sends the audio from the previous state to an Amazon Lex bot.
- **Play response – Start speech** plays the audio response from the previous state. Transition to **Wait**.

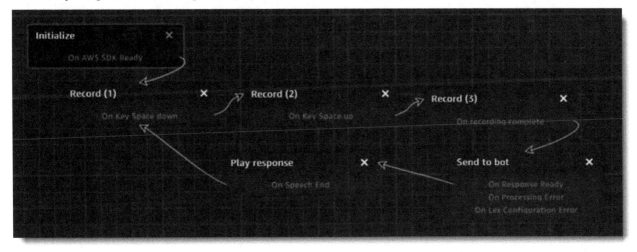

Script

You can use a script to update the configuration of an entity's dialogue component in response to user input. The following example adds a listener to two buttons to change the active bot when a button is clicked.

Example Script – Add Event Listener to Buttons

- **Entity** – Host or other entity with a dialogue component.

```
1 'use strict';
2
3 function setup(args, ctx) {
4   ctx.entityData.changeBot = function(event){
5     var name = event.target.getAttribute("botname");
6     var alias = event.target.getAttribute("botalias");
7     ctx.entity.dialogueComponent.updateConfig({name: name, alias: alias})
8   };
9   document.getElementById("bot1button").addEventListener('click', ctx.entityData.changeBot);
10  document.getElementById("bot2button").addEventListener('click', ctx.entityData.changeBot);
11 }
```

Example HTML 3D component – Buttons

```
1  <style>
2  button {
3    background-color: #4CAF50;
4    border: none;
5    color: white;
6    padding: 15px 25px;
7    text-align: center;
8    font-size: 16px;
9    cursor: pointer;
10 }
11
12 button:hover {
13   background-color: green;
14 }
15 </style>
16
17 <button id="bot1button" botname="OrderFlowers" botalias="latest" type="button">Order Flowers</
     button>
18 <button id="bot2button" botname="BookTrip" botalias="latest" type="button">Book Trip</button>
```

Amazon Sumerian 2D Graphics Component

A two-dimensional image or video.

Properties

- **Tint** – The tint color.
- **Emissiveness** – The emissiveness of the image.
- **Opacity** – The opacity of the image.
- **Reflection** – The reflectivity of the image.

Amazon Sumerian HTML Components

You can use the Amazon Sumerian HTML components to quickly add text and images to your scene. The **HTML** component overlays a 2D window that maintains the same orientation (camera facing) at all times. The **HTML 3D** component is a 3D object within the scene and can be viewed from different angles as the camera moves around it.

Note

HTML 3D works well in 2D scenes and in VR with some limitations. HTML 2D doesn't work in VR, and appears as a black box in VR mode. Scene contents between an entity with an HTML 3D component and the camera are rendered normally. However, nothing behind an HTML 3D component is visible, so HTML components should not use transparency.

You can use style attributes on your HTML elements, or include a separate `style` tag that defines styles.

HTML 2D Component

The HTML component adds a 2D HTML document (a `div`) to the scene, and you can edit its content in the text editor. You can position the document using the entity transform, or use CSS to position it relative to the viewport.

Properties

- **Move with transform** – Position the HTML document within the scene using the transform component on the same entity. The document is always the same size and faces the camera, but can move relative to the camera. To position the HTML content relative to the viewport, deselect this option and set positioning with a style attribute.
- **Pixel perfect** – When positioning with the entity transform, snap the HTML window to the closest pixel position.
- **Attributes** – Add HTML attributes to the bounding `div` tag. For example, you can add a style attribute to position the HTML content onscreen.

Choose the **Open in editor** button to open the HTML document in the text editor.

Example Video Window

HTML properties

- **Attributes** – style: position:absolute;right:50px;bottom:50px

```
1 <iframe width="100%" height="100%" src="https://www.youtube.com/embed/DqeUFGpZLUw" frameborder
    ="0" allow="autoplay; encrypted-media" allowfullscreen></iframe>
```

HTML 3D Component

The HTML 3D component adds a screen-like element to an entity that you can position in the scene. You set the size of the screen by using the X and Y scale on the transform component. The width and height properties determine how much content (in pixels) fits in that space.

Properties

- **Width** – The width of the HTML content, in pixels. The height of the content is determined by the entity's Y scale.

Example Movie Screen

Transform

- **Translation** – X: 1, Y: 5, Z: -20
- **Scale** – X: 16, Y: 9, Z: 1

HTML 3D properties

- **Width** – 1920. Height is automatically set to 1080 (1920 * 9 / 16).

```
1 <iframe width="100%" height="100%" src="https://www.youtube.com/embed/DqeUFGpZLUw" frameborder
    ="0" allow="autoplay; encrypted-media" allowfullscreen></iframe>
```

In the rendered scene, your HTML content is placed within a div with a white background that is transformed with CSS 3D. You can't modify style or other attributes on the div directly. To ensure that your content fills the component, place it within a div with height and width set to 100%.

In VR mode, HTML 3D components are rendered at a very low frame rate. It isn't suited for video, or any content that is updated frequently or in response to user input. For more information, see Understanding Amazon Sumerian's HTML 3D Component on the Sumerian website.

Using HTML Components with Scripts

You can interact with content in HTML components by using standard JavaScript and HTML DOM events.

The following example HTML and script add buttons that the user can click to change the active Amazon Lex chatbot on a host with a dialogue component.

Example HTML 3D component – Buttons

```
1  <style>
2  button {
3    background-color: #4CAF50;
4    border: none;
5    color: white;
6    padding: 15px 25px;
7    text-align: center;
8    font-size: 16px;
9    cursor: pointer;
10  }
11
12  button:hover {
13    background-color: green;
14  }
15  </style>
```

```
16
17  <button id="bot1button" botname="OrderFlowers" botalias="latest" type="button">Order Flowers</
        button>
18  <button id="bot2button" botname="BookTrip" botalias="latest" type="button">Book Trip</button>
```

Example Script – Add Event Listener to Buttons

- **Entity** – Host or other entity with a dialogue component.

```
1   'use strict';
2
3   function setup(args, ctx) {
4     ctx.entityData.changeBot = function(event){
5       var name = event.target.getAttribute("botname");
6       var alias = event.target.getAttribute("botalias");
7       ctx.entity.dialogueComponent.updateConfig({name: name, alias: alias})
8     };
9     document.getElementById("bot1button").addEventListener('click', ctx.entityData.changeBot);
10    document.getElementById("bot2button").addEventListener('click', ctx.entityData.changeBot);
11  }
```

Amazon Sumerian Sound Component

The sound component adds a number of sound assets to the entity. The sound will not play automatically, but you can play it using a script or the state machine.

Properties

- **Master volume** – The volume of all sounds in the component.

Amazon Sumerian Light Component

The light component adds a light source to the entity.

Properties

- **Type**
    - **Point** – Emit light in all directions from a point in space, like a flame.
    - **Directional** – Emit light uniformly over the entire scene, like the sun.
    - **Spot** – Emit light in a cone, like a spotlight.
- **Color** – The color of the light.
- **Intensity** – The intensity of the light (typically between 0 and 1).
- **Specular** – The intensity of the specular light (typically between 0 and 1).
- **Range** (point and spot) –
- **Cone angle** (spot) – The angle of the cone at the light source, in degrees.
- **Penumbra** (spot) – The intensity of the light near the edges of the cone.
- **Projection** (directional and spot) – Upload a texture to apply to the light.
- **Shadows** (directional and spot) – Cast shadows from objects that the light hits.

Amazon Sumerian Particle System Component

The particle system component simulates fluid entities such as liquids, clouds, and flames by generating and animating large numbers of small 2D images in the scene.

Properties

- **General** – The basic behavior of the particle emitter.
    - **Auto play** – Start the emission animation when the scene starts.
    - **Loop** – Loop the animation.
    - **Duration** – Duration of the animation in seconds.
    - **Prewarm** – Load the effect prior to playback.
    - **Max particles** – Limit the number of visible particles.
    - **Gravity** – Vector of the gravity force that applies to particles.
    - **Seed** – Randomization seed. Experiment with values to find a look that you like, or set to -1 to get a different effect each time.
    - **Local space simulation** – Set to true to simulate the particle system within the boundaries of the parent entity, instead of in the entire scene.
- **Emitter shape** – The shape and size of the emitter. Additional settings are specific to each shape.

Box

- **Random direction** – Emit each particle in a random direction.
- **Box extents** – The height, width, and length of the emitter.

Sphere

- **Radius** – The size of the emitter.
- **Emit from shell** – Emit particles from the outside edge of the emitter.
- **Random direction** – Emit each particle in a random direction.

Cone

- **Random direction** – Emit each particle in a random direction.
- **Emit from** – Emit particles from the narrow end of the cone (**Base**), the center of the cone (**Volume**), or the edges of the cone (**Volumeedge**).
- **Cone radius** – The radius of the cone at the narrow end.
- **Cone angle** – The angle at which the sides of the cone flare out.
- **Cone length** – The length of the sides of the cone.
- **Over duration properties** – Fine tune values that apply to each loop of animation. Each value can be constant, or progress linearly or randomly over the duration.
    - **Emission rate** – The number of particles emitted per second.
    - **Start speed** – The speed of the particles.
    - **Start size** – The size of the particles.
    - **Start color** – The color of the particles.
    - **Start life time** – The number of seconds before each particle disappears.
    - **Start angle** – The angle of particles.
- **Over lifetime properties** – Fine tune values that apply to the entire lifetime of the particle emitter. Each value can be constant, or progress linearly or randomly over the lifetime.
    - **Color** – The color of the particles. Compounds with the duration color.
    - **Size** – The size of the particles. Compounds with the duration size.
    - **Rotation speed** – Rotation of particles in degrees per second.
    - **Local velocity** – Local space velocity in units per second.
    - **World velocity** – World space velocity in units per second.
- **Texture** – The texture of each particle. Use one of the provided textures or choose **custom** to upload a texture.
- **Texture animation**
    - **Texture tiles** – The number of tiles in the sprite sheet, in X and Y directions.

- **Cycles** – The number of texture animation cycles to finish over the lifetime.
- **Frame over lifetime** – A curve specifying when to show which frame in the animation. 0 is the first frame and 1 is the last. A linear curve starting at 0 and ending at 1 traverses all frames in the animation.
- **Rendering** – Customize the rendering behavior.
  - **Billboard** – Particles always face the camera.
  - **Render queue** – Render queue of the particle mesh.
  - **Render queue offset** – Offset added to the render queue.
  - **Blending** – The type of blending (**None, Additive, Subtractive, Multiply,** or **Transparency**).
  - **Depth write** – Write to the depth buffer.
  - **Depth test** – Test against the depth buffer.
  - **Sorting mode** – The draw order for particles (**None** or **Camera distance**). For transparency blending, camera distance sorting is recommended.
  - **Opacity threshold** – The lower alpha threshold at which fragments are discarded.

Amazon Sumerian Animation Component

The animation component controls the animations of an imported 3D mesh. It contains a list of *animation states* and *transitions*.

When you import your model into the editor, you get a geometry component and an animation component.

The animation **State** contains information about an animation, such as how many times it should loop, how fast it should run, and if it has any transition. If there's no transition for an animation state, the default transitions at the bottom are used.

If you want to switch between animation states, but want the transition between them to be smooth, add a **Transition**.

Transitions

- **Fade** – A transition that blends over a given time from one animation state to another, beginning the target clip from local time 0 at the start of the transition. This is best used with two clips that have similar motions.
- **SyncFade** – A transition that blends over a given time from one animation state to another, synchronizing the target state to the initial state's start time. This is best used with two clips that have similar motions.
- **Frozen** – A two-state transition that freezes the starting state at its current position and blends that over time with a target state. The target state moves forward in time during the blend as normal.

Amazon Sumerian Collider Component

The collider component adds collision geometry to the entity. If used together with a rigid body component, you can create a dynamic, colliding entity. If the collider doesn't have any rigid body component, it becomes a static collision geometry in the physics world. We call this a *static collider*.

If the entity with a collider or any of its parents has a dynamic rigid body component, it will turn into a *dynamic collider*. If the entity with a collider or any of its parents has a kinematic rigid body component, it will turn into a *kinematic collider*.

The collider shapes are rendered with a green wireframe.

Properties

- **Shape** – The shape of the collider.

    - Box
    - Sphere
    - Plane
    - Infinite plane

- **Trigger** –

    If the collider is not a trigger, it emits these events during collisions:

    - sumerian.physics.beginContact
    - sumerian.physics.duringContact
    - sumerian.physics.endContact

    Trigger messages are sent upon collision

	Static Collider	Rigidbody Collider	Kinematic Rigidbody Collider	Static Trigger Collider	Rigidbody Trigger Collider	Kinematic Rigidbody Trigger Collider
Static Collider					Y	
Rigidbody Collider				Y	Y	Y
Kinematic Rigidbody Collider					Y	
Static Trigger Collider		Y			Y	
Rigidbody Trigger Collider	Y	Y	Y	Y	Y	Y
Kinematic Rigidbody Trigger Collider		Y			Y	

    If the collider is a trigger, it will *not* collide with other physics objects. However, it will emit events when a physics object enters it. Available events are:

    - sumerian.physics.triggerEnter
    - sumerian.physics.triggerStay
    - sumerian.physics.triggerLeave

Collision detection occurs and messages are sent upon collision

	Static Collider	Rigidbody Collider	Kinematic Rigidbody Collider	Static Trigger Collider	Rigidbody Trigger Collider	Kinematic Rigidbody Trigger Collider
Static Collider		Y				
Rigidbody Collider	Y	Y	Y			
Kinematic Rigidbody Collider		Y				
Static Trigger Collider						
Rigidbody Trigger Collider						
Kinematic Rigidbody Trigger Collider						

- **Friction** – 0 Means no friction. The final friction (and restitution) value used in a collision is computed using multiplication. For example, a sphere with friction=0.5 that collides with a plane with friction=0.5 will get a friction value of 0.25.

- **Restitution** – How much the collider should bounce. 0 is no bounce and 1 is maximum bounce. If you set restitution to a number larger than one, it gains more and more energy for each bounce.

- **Half extents** – The collider's half extents on the X, Y, and Z axises.

Amazon Sumerian Rigid Body Component

The rigid body component adds physics properties, such as mass and velocity, to the entity. The component will simulate physics for the component and set the position and orientation of the entity accordingly.

Properties

- **Mass** – The mass of the body.
- **Kinematic** – Make the rigid body kinematic instead of dynamic. A dynamic body is affected by external forces such as gravity. Kinematic bodies do not fall or react when hit.
- **Velocity** – The initial linear velocity of the body.
- **Angular velocity** – The initial angular velocity of the body
- **Linear drag** – Resistance of the body to linear movement, between 0 and 1.
- **Angular drag** – Resistance of the body to angular movement, between 0 and 1.

If you add a collider component to the entity, the collider is used for rigid body collision, with the center of mass being at the same location as the rigid body.

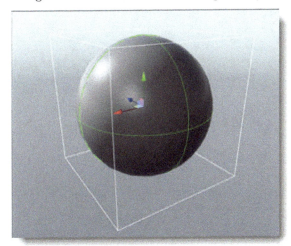

Adding a single collider component and a rigid body component on the same entity is a bit limited. The collider will always be centered in the entity and you cannot move it. The solution is to put it on an entity below the rigid body component in the hierarchy. This lets you move the collider or use multiple colliders.

So if you'd like to make a chair consisting out of six colliders (four legs + back rest + seat), you first create a root entity with a rigid body component. Then you create six entities with box collider components and put them as children of the root entity. Scale and position them correctly, and you're done.

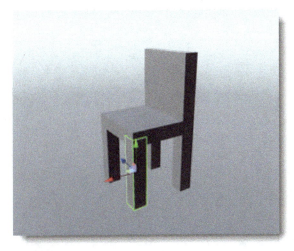

Amazon Sumerian State Machine Component

The state machine component adds a Sumerian state machine to the entity. You can use state machines to create dynamic and interactive scenes that feature animation, physics, special effects. State machines are specific to an entity, so you can have multiple state machines in your scene that trigger on different events.

A state machine has one or more *behaviors* that organize scene logic into *states*, *actions*, and *transitions*. See Amazon Sumerian State Machines for more information.

Amazon Sumerian Script Component

You can add scripts to any entity. A script component can contain multiple scripts. Scripts run in order from top to bottom and you can adjust the order in the script component properties.

To support reuse, you add an instance of a script to the script component, not the script itself. The instance contains the state and parameters of the script, letting you add multiple instances of the same script with different behavior on each, based on the arguments provided.

Properties

- **Enabled** – Clear the check box to disable a script.
- **Instance of** – Each script instance in the list has a reference to the script it is using. Choose a script to go to the script's own panel.
- **Parameters** – Any parameters defined in the script's `parameters` array appear here. Adjust the values to customize the behavior of this script instance.

To structure your parameters, you can store them in a JSON file. Start by defining the parameters in the script itself. Then add the JSON file and reference it from the script settings.

Example Script with JSON parameter

```
1 varsetup=function(args,ctx){
2   console.log(args.myJsonParameter);// Prints the parsed JSON data
3 };
4
5 var parameters=[{
6   key:'myJsonParameter',
7   type:'json'
8 }];
```

To create a script with JSON parameters

1. Create a blank entity.

2. Choose **Add component**, and then choose **Script**.

3. Choose **Add script**, and then choose **Custom**.

4. Choose **Edit script**.

5. Replace the default `parameters` declaration with the following.

```
1 var parameters=[{
2   key:'myJsonParameter',
3   type:'json'
4 }];
```

6. Return to the script settings. The settings automatically update to include the JSON parameter.

7. Drop a JSON file in the parameter field.

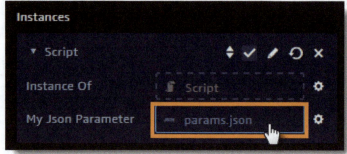

Amazon Sumerian Timeline Component

Use timelines to move, rotate, or change the scale of entities over time. You can set the start and end values of these properties, and add keyframes to control the speed or direction of the animation along the way. The timeline can also emit custom events, which can be consumed from a state machine or script.

To create a timeline, choose **Create entity, Timeline**. You can also add the timeline component to an existing entity, but don't add it to the entity that you want to animate. The timeline can only control entities other than the one to which it is attached.

Properties

- **Duration** – Length of the timeline, in seconds.
- **Loop** – Enable to repeat the timeline animation in a loop.
- **Auto start** – To trigger the timeline with a state machine or script, disable this option to prevent the timeline from starting automatically in playback mode.

To open the timeline editor, choose **Toggle timeline** in the timeline component, or choose **Timeline** from the **Tools** menu.

To add entities to the timeline, drag them from the entities panel onto the timeline editor. Each *channel* in the editor controls one property of the transform, such as the X translation or the Z scale. Click the clock icon next to a property to enable the channel and add the first keyframe.

Add more keyframes to a channel by choosing a time and changing the property's value. During playback, the entity animates between the transform values at each keyframe. By default, changing a property's value automatically creates a keyframe. You can disable this by clicking the key icon next to the **Drop entity here** box.

Add **Event channels** to the timeline to emit custom events onto the system bus. The name of the channel is the name of the event that Sumerian emits at each keyframe on the event channel. Consume this event from a script with SystemBus.addListener, or from a state machine with the **Listen action**.

Amazon Sumerian Assets

The assets panel in Sumerian collects shareable assets in the scene. When you add an asset to a scene, Sumerian automatically adds it to a *default pack* in the assets panel. Entities that you create are not automatically added, but you can drag them from the entities panel into the assets panel to create an entity asset.

Asset Types

- **Entity** – A Sumerian entity. If you import a file or asset pack, drop the entity from the assets panel onto the canvas to add it to your scene.

- **Mesh** – A polygon mesh from a 3D model.

- **Skeleton** – A skeleton and animations from a 3D model.

- **Material** – A material component with textures for each renderable layer generated from a 3D model.

- **Sound** – An audio file for use with a sound component.

- **Script** – A JavaScript script that can be instantiated on a script component.

- **Speech** – A text file for use with a speech component.

- **JSON** – A JSON file that can be used as a parameter input on a script component.

- **Skybox** – A collection of textures that can be added to the background of the scene in the scene's environment settings.

- **Behavior** – A collection of actions that can be added to a state machine component.

- **Texture** – An image file that can be added to layers of a material component, a 2D graphics component, or a skybox.

To add an asset to a scene, you can drag it from your desktop directly onto the canvas. Depending on the file type, the editor creates an entity in the entities panel, and one or more assets. For example, when you add a JPG image to a scene, you get an image entity in the scene, a material asset, and a texture asset.

To add an asset to a scene

1. Open a scene in the Sumerian editor.

2. Drag a file from your desktop file browser onto the canvas.

   or

   Create a blank asset by clicking the plus icon next to the default pack. To see the icon, select the pack name.

3. Choose the asset in the assets panel and modify it by using the options in the inspector panel.

Amazon Sumerian Asset Packs

You can organize your assets and share them between scenes by creating a *pack*. Create a pack in the assets panel and move or copy assets into it.

Packs support the following actions:

- ![+ icon] – Create a new asset in the pack.
- ![export icon] – Export the pack to the asset library.
- ![brush icon] – Delete any assets in the pack that are not used in the scene.
- ![trash icon] – Delete the asset pack.

Exporting a pack adds it to the project that you choose. If you don't have a project yet, create one in the dashboard. You can then use the dashboard to copy or move the pack to a different scene or project. Exported packs are not tied to the in-scene pack or its assets.

To add an asset to a pack and export it

1. Open a scene in the Sumerian editor.

2. Under **Assets**, choose **Create pack**.

3. Choose the pack and modify the name, description, tags, and custom attributes in the inspector panel.

4. Drag an asset from the default pack into the custom pack.

   or

   Duplicate the item by selecting it and then clicking the duplicate icon. Drag the duplicate into the custom pack.

5. Select the custom pack, and then click the asset library icon ![asset library icon], or choose **Add to asset library** in the inspector panel.

6. Choose an asset type for the asset pack.

7. Choose **Add to asset library**.

8. Choose a project, and then choose **Select**.

Amazon Sumerian Scene Templates

Sumerian provides scene templates that you can use as a starting point for your scene.

Sumerian Scene Templates

- **Augmented reality** – Template for creating augmented reality (AR) scenes with a companion sample app. See Amazon Sumerian Augmented Reality Tools for more information.
- **Default lighting** – An empty scene with a skysphere and three directional lights. This template is used in the interface tutorial.
- **Speech & gestures** – Scene with a Sumerian host configured to use speech with a state machine.

Choose any of these templates in the dashboard to create a draft scene.

Amazon Sumerian Virtual Reality Tools

Sumerian provides a pack of virtual reality (VR)-related assets to make it easy to enable VR in your scene. The asset pack includes a VR camera that lets the user enter VR mode, and VR controllers for interacting with the environment.

Supported VR Headsets

- Oculus Rift
- Oculus Go
- HTC Vive
- HTC Vive Pro
- Lenovo Mirage Solo

To enable VR in your scene

1. Open a scene in the Sumerian editor.

2. Choose **Import assets**.

3. Choose **CoreVR**, and then choose **Add**.

4. When the asset pack finishes loading, drag the **VRCameraRig** entity onto the canvas to add it to your scene.

5. Choose the **VRCameraRig** entity.

6. Choose the **VRCameraRig** component.

7. Choose the **Current VR camera rig** option to enable the rig.

When a user enters VR mode with a headset and controllers attached, the HMD camera tracks the headset, and the VR controllers track the controllers in 3D space. The VR camera rig manages the other entities and enables the VR mode button in the scene.

Only the controllers of the type attached are rendered in the scene, so you can leave all of the included entities attached to support both types. You can also replace the included controller models with your own.

See Getting Started with VR for a tutorial that uses these assets.

Amazon Sumerian Augmented Reality Tools

Sumerian provides a template, assets, and sample projects that you can use to develop augmented reality (AR) applications for iOS and Android devices.

The **Augmented Reality** scene template is available in the dashboard. Use it as a starting point for your augmented reality scene.

The scene includes the following resources:

- **AR Camera** – The main camera, with a script that maps it to the device's camera.
- **AR Camera Control** – A script that uses the Sumerian engine AR System to access the device's augmented reality API. You can view this script in the text editor.
- **ARAnchor** – An empty entity that the AR app uses to anchor objects in the scene to the real world.

You can construct an AR scene from this template by adding models and making them children of the **ARAnchor** entity. Publish the scene, and then use the sample AR Kit project to build an app that uses it.

Topics

- Android Sample Project
- iOS Sample Project

Android Sample Project

The sample project, amazon-sumerian-arcore-starter-app, is an Android Studio project with an ARCore app that loads a scene created with the AR template. Replace the scene URL in the view controller with the URL of your published scene, build the app, and then run it on a compatible Android device to see it in action.

See the Augmented Reality Using Sumerian and ARCore tutorial to explore how to use these assets.

iOS Sample Project

The sample project, amazon-sumerian-arkit-starter-app, is an XCode project with a Swift app that loads a scene created with the AR template. Replace the scene URL in the view controller with the URL of your published scene, build the app, and then run it on a compatible iOS device to see it in action.

See the Augmented Reality Using Sumerian and ARKit tutorial to explore how to use these assets.

Amazon Sumerian Hosts

A host is a asset provided by Sumerian that has built in animation, speech, and behavior for interacting with users. Use hosts to engage users in conversation and convey information.

To add a host to your scene

1. Open a scene in the Sumerian editor.

2. Choose **Import assets**.

3. Choose one of the following hosts:

    - **Cristine**
    - **Preston**
    - **Luke**

4. Choose **Add**.

5. Drag the host entity from the assets panel onto the canvas.

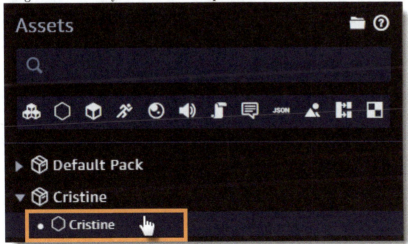

All of a host's meshes, materials, animations, and scripts are bundled into a single entity with three configurable components:

- **Transform** – The host's location relative to the scene or its parent entity.
- **Host** – Animation and behavior settings.
- **Speech** – Text-to-speech capability with Amazon Polly.

Models and animations for hosts are locked. You cannot modify or extend them.

Models

Drop a model file on the assets panel to import it. When you import a model, Sumerian converts it into an asset pack that contains the model's meshes, skeletons, materials, and textures. Meshes are triangulated automatically during import. The process can take some time, depending on the model size and format.

You can import models up to 50 MB in size in the following formats.

File Formats

- **FilmBox** – .fbx

  www.autodesk.com/products/fbx/overview

- **Wavefront OBJ** – .obj

  en.wikipedia.org/wiki/Wavefront_.obj_file

After the model is imported, drop the model entity from the asset pack onto the canvas. This adds one or more entities to the scene in a hierarchy based on the imported file. At a minimum, the entity has transform, geometry, and material components. If you import a model that has a skeleton and animations, you also get an animation component. The skeleton and polygon mesh are attached to the geometry component, and textures are attached to the material component.

To optimize the model importing process, remove unneeded data by deleting the object history and freezing transformations in your modeling tool. If you can, avoid using geometric transformations. If your model has animations, bake them into the model and avoid using constraints.

The Sumerian engine supports the following model features.

Model Features

- **Vertex colors** – Per-vertex colors or per-face-vertex colors are supported.

  When the mesh data contains vertex colors, a slider is available on the mesh's material panel under the diffuse channel. You can use the slider to blend between the set diffuse map or color and the vertex color.

- **UV maps** – If two are available, you can use the second one, for example, for light maps or ambient occlusion maps.

  In the editor, you are able to apply these textures on the ambient channel in the material panel.

- **Tangents** – If no tangent data is provided, it is generated during the conversion.

- **Normals** – If no normal data is provided, interpolated normals are generated during the conversion.

- **Skeleton animations** – Animation via skeleton mesh deformation is supported. You can provide several animations in one file.

  Shader limitations

  - The maximum number of weights per vertex is 4. If more are provided, the ones with the least values are removed.
  - Keeping the joint count low enables the support of a broader set of hardware.

  If you have already converted a model with skeleton animations into the editor, and later add more animations in your modeling tool, you can add those new animations onto the existing model in the editor.

  You do this by dropping the file on the animation panel's animation state drop area. This issues the file upload as usual, but during conversion, only the animation data is exported. The underlying skeleton rig must be the same for this to work. If you changed the rig, you must reimport the model through the regular process.

- **Embedded textures (FBX)** – When exporting to the FBX binary format, you can embed textures into the resulting file.

Skybox

A skybox is a texture that you apply to the background of a scene to show the sky, space, or an enclosing structure. A skybox can be a single texture that wraps onto a sphere, or six textures that wrap onto a cube. Add a skybox to your scene in the scene's environment settings.

To create a skybox

1. Open a scene in the Sumerian editor.

2. Click the plus icon next to the default pack. To see the icon, select the pack name.

3. Choose **Skybox**.

4. Choose the shape of the skybox.

Skybox Shapes

- **Box** – Six square images that map onto a cube (cube map).
- **Sphere** – A single rectangular image that maps onto a sphere (equirectangular projection).

1. Drop a texture asset or image file on each section of the skybox.

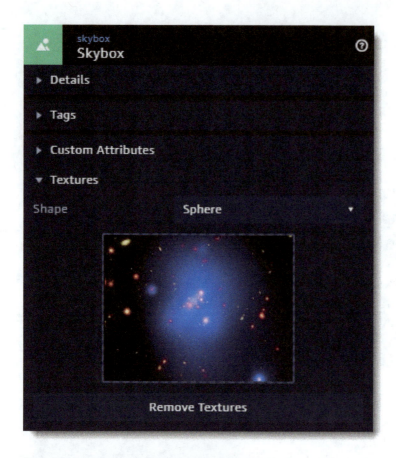

2. Choose the root node in the **Entities** panel.

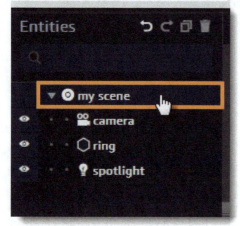

3. Choose **Environment**.

4. Drop the skybox asset from the assets panel onto the **Skybox** field.

Media

You can import media files into Sumerian to use as textures, audio, or text objects. Sumerian supports the following file formats.

Textures up to 10 MB

- CRN
- DDS
- JPG, JPEG
- PNG
- SVG
- TGA
- MP4
- OGV
- WEBM

Audio up to 10 MB

- OGG
- MP3
- WAVE, WAV

Text up to 1 MB

- JS
- JSON

You can combine multiple asset files into a ZIP archive up to 200 MB in size, as long as each file meets the size requirement for its type when decompressed.

Amazon Sumerian State Machines

Amazon Sumerian behaviors are state machines that you can attach to the state machine component on an entity. A behavior is a collection of *states* that transition between one another based on user interaction, timing, or other events.

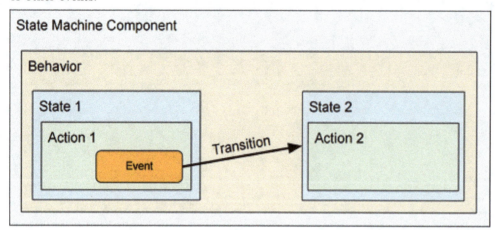

Each state in a behavior consists of one or more *actions* that contain some logic that Sumerian defines. An action on the active state can do things like respond to a user clicking the entity that the behavior is attached to, run a script, or record audio and send it to an Amazon Lex chatbot.

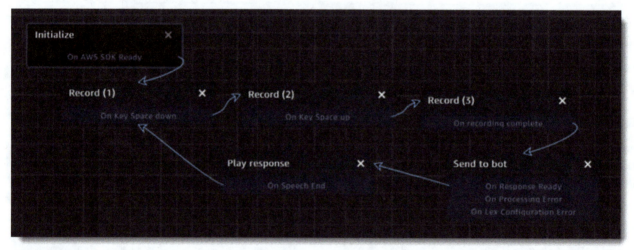

All actions on a state execute simultaneously when the state is entered. If an action has a built-in transition, the transition enters the next state when the action is complete. Some actions modify the entity or scene and don't have a built-in transition. Others perform a calculation or wait for an event, and then fire a transition.

In the previous example, the first state waits for the AWS SDK to get credentials and signal that it's ready. When this occurs, it transitions to a state that waits for the user to press the Spacebar. This transitions to another state that has two actions: one starts recording audio, and a second waits for the user to release the key. When the user releases the key, another state stops the audio recording and transitions to a fifth state that sends the recorded audio to an Amazon Lex chatbot.

The chatbot action has three transitions, and can respond differently depending on the result of the call to Amazon Lex. Finally, the sixth state plays the audio response from the chatbot and transitions back to the second state to wait for another key press. For more information on this example, see Amazon Sumerian Dialogue Component.

Sumerian provides many actions, organized into the following categories.

Topics

- Animation State Machine Actions in Amazon Sumerian
- Audio and Camera State Machine Actions in Amazon Sumerian
- AWS Feature State Machine Actions in Amazon Sumerian
- Keyboard and Mouse State Machine Actions in Amazon Sumerian
- Effects and Lighting State Machine Actions in Amazon Sumerian
- Materials and Rendering State Machine Actions in Amazon Sumerian
- Physics and Collision State Machine Actions in Amazon Sumerian
- Logic and Transition State Machine Actions in Amazon Sumerian

Animation State Machine Actions in Amazon Sumerian

You can use state machine actions to animate and transform entities in Sumerian.

Transform actions change the translation, rotation, and scale of the entity. Tween actions change the same values smoothly over a configurable amount of time.

Transform Actions

- **Look at** – Rotate the entity to face a point in space.
- **Tween look at** – Smoothly rotate the entity to face a point in space over time.
- **Face current camera** – Rotate the entity to face the active camera.
- **Move** – Move the entity.
- **Tween move** – Smoothly move the entity over time.
- **Rotate** – Change the entity's rotation values.
- **Tween rotate** – Smoothly rotate the entity over time.
- **Scale** – Change the entity's scale values.
- **Tween scale** – Smoothly scale the entity over time.
- **Shake** – Shake the entity.

Animation actions control the entity's animation component.

Animation Actions

- **Copy joint transform** – Copy a joint transform from another entity, and apply it to this entity. This entity must be a child of an entity with an animation component.
- **Pause animation** – Pause skeleton animation.
- **Resume animation** – Continue playing skeleton animation.
- **Set animation** – Transition to a selected animation.
- **Set animation offset** – Change the animation clip offset.
- **Set animation time scale** – Change the time scale for the current animation.

Host actions configure a Sumerian host to play an emote or look at another entity.

Host Actions

- **Play emote** – Play a host emote.
- **Set point of interest target** – Change the target entity of a host.

Audio and Camera State Machine Actions in Amazon Sumerian

You can use state machine actions in Amazon Sumerian to control audio settings and the scene camera.

Audio actions

Audio Actions

- **Mute**, **Toggle mute**, and **Unmute** – Mute or unmute all sounds in the scene. **Toggle mute** mutes if sound is currently unmuted and vice-versa.
- **Play sound**, **Pause sound**, and **Stop sound** – Play, pause, or stop a sound from the entity's sound component.
- **Sound fade in** and **Sound fade out** – Start or stop a sound with a fade.
- **Start microphone recording** – Start recording audio from microphone input.
- **Stop microphone recording** – Stop recording audio from microphone input and store it on the entity. The audio can then be used by the Send audio input to dialogue bot action.

Camera actions interact with the entity's camera component.

Camera Actions

- **Dolly zoom** – Perform a dolly zoom.
- **Switch camera** – Switch to a different camera.

AWS Feature State Machine Actions in Amazon Sumerian

You can use state machine actions to control AWS features integrated with Amazon Sumerian.

AWS Feature Actions

- **AWS SDK ready** – Wait for the AWS SDK for JavaScript to get credentials before using features that call AWS services. See Configuring AWS Credentials for Your Amazon Sumerian Scene for details.
- **Change speech volume** – Change the volume of the entity's speech component.
- **Send audio input to dialogue bot** – Send recorded audio to the Amazon Lex chatbot assigned to the entity's dialogue component.
- **Send text input to dialogue bot** – Send text input to the Amazon Lex chatbot assigned to the entity's dialogue component.
- **Start speech** and **Stop speech**– Play or stop a speech component.

Keyboard and Mouse State Machine Actions in Amazon Sumerian

You can use state machine actions in Amazon Sumerian to respond to keyboard, mouse, and touch events.

Keyboard actions transition in response to a specific key press. You can add multiple keyboard actions to the same state to respond to multiple inputs. The first key press that satisfies any keyboard action on the state triggers a transition to the next state.

Keyboard Actions

- **Key down** – Press a key.
- **Key up** – Release a key.
- **Key pressed** – Press a key.
- **Arrow key** – Press up, down, left, or right on the arrow keys.
- **WASD key** – Press W, A, S, or D.

Mouse actions listen for click, hover, and touch events on the entity or its children, and then transition to a new state.

Mouse Actions

- **Click or tap on entity** – Choose an entity by clicking or tapping it.
- **Hover enter** – Move the mouse cursor over an entity.
- **Hover exit** – Move the mouse cursor off of an entity.
- **Mouse move** – Move the mouse cursor.
- **Mouse down or touch start** – Press a mouse button, or touch the screen. Has separate transitions for touch and each mouse button.
- **Mouse up or touch end** – Release a mouse button, or stop touching the screen. Has separate transitions for touch and each mouse button.
- **Mouse pressed** – Press a mouse button. Choose **Left**, **Middle**, or **Right**. Has one transition for the selected button.
- **Pick** – Click or tap an entity and then release, without moving away from the entity.
- **Pick and exit** – Click or tap an entity, and then release to open a link in a new window.

Effects and Lighting State Machine Actions in Amazon Sumerian

You can use state machine actions in Amazon Sumerian to modify scene lighting or add special effects.

Effects and Lighting Actions

- **Add light** – Add a point light to the entity.
- **Set light properties** – Modify a light component's properties.
- **Remove light** – Remove the entity's light component.
- **Tween light** – Smoothly transition between two light colors.
- **Fire FX** – Make the entity emit fire. To extinguish the fire, use the **Remove particles** action.
- **Smoke FX** – Make an entity emit smoke. To cancel the smoke emitter, use the **Remove particles** action.
- **Start particle system** and **Stop particle system** – Start or stop a particle emitter.
- **Pause particle system** – Pause a particle system.
- **Remove particles** – Remove any particle emitter attached to the entity
- **Toggle post effects** – Enable or disable all post effects in the scene.

Materials and Rendering State Machine Actions in Amazon Sumerian

You can use state machine actions in Amazon Sumerian to modify entity textures and visibility.

Materials and Rendering Actions

- **Hide** and **Show** – Hide or show the entity and its children.
- **Set material color** – Change the color of the entity's material.
- **Set render target** – Render what a camera sees on the entity's texture.
- **Sprite animation** – Start a sprite animation.
- **Tween material color** – Smoothly change the material color.
- **Tween material opacity** – Smoothly change the material's opacity.
- **Tween texture offset** – Smoothly change the material texture offset.

Physics and Collision State Machine Actions in Amazon Sumerian

You can use state machine actions in Amazon Sumerian to apply physics and check for collisions.

Physics actions move an object by simulating real-world physics.

Physics Actions

- **Apply force on rigid body** – Apply a force to the entity's rigid body.
- **Apply impulse on rigid body** – Apply an impulse to the entity's rigid body.
- **Apply torque on rigid body** – Apply a torque to the entity's rigid body.
- **Set rigid body angular velocity** – Change the angular velocity of a rigid body.
- **Set rigid body position** – Change the position of a rigid body.
- **Set rigid body rotation** – Change the rotation of a rigid body.
- **Set rigid body velocity** – Change the velocity of a rigid body.

Collision actions detect changes in an object's position and transition to a new state.

Collision Actions

- **Camera distance** – The entity is at a distance from the current camera or a point in space.
- **In box** – The entity is within a box bounded by two points at opposite corners.
- **Trigger enter** – The entity's collider enters a trigger volume.
- **Trigger leave** – The entity's collider leaves a trigger volume.

Logic and Transition State Machine Actions in Amazon Sumerian

You can use state machine actions in Amazon Sumerian to run scripts, respond to events, and add transitions to a state.

Logic actions perform calculations, run scripts, or interact with the page document.

Logic Actions

- **Compare counter** and **Compare 2 counters** – Compare a counter with a set value, or compare the value of two counters.
- **DOM listen** – Add a DOM event listener on one or many elements (specified by a query selector), and perform a transition on a given event.
- **Emit message** – Emit a message (a ping) to a channel on the bus. Messages can be listened to by the **Listen** transition action, or by scripts using the `SystemBus.addListener(channel, callback)` function.
- **Execute script** – Run a script, and transition on success or failure. Use the `enter` and `exit` functions in your script to run code when the state is entered and exited. To trigger a transition, call `ctx.transitions.success()` or `ctx.transitions.failure()` on the context object.
- **Execute script condition** – Evaluate an expression, and transition on a true or false result.
- **Execute script expression** – Execute a statement.
- **Get HTML text** and **Set HTML text** – Read or change the contents of an HTML element.
- **Increment counter** – Increment a counter with a value.
- **Log message** – Print a message in the debug console of your browser.
- **Set counter** – Change a counter to a value.
- **Toggle full screen** – Expand the scene to fill the screen. For browsers to allow this, the previous state must have a Click or tap on entity action that transitions to the state that runs this action.

Timeline actions interact with the entity's timeline component.

Timeline Actions

- **Pause timeline** – Pause a timeline.
- **Set timelime time** – Jump to a point on a timeline.
- **Start timeline** and **Stop timeline** – Start or stop a timeline.

Transition actions move from one state to another. Many actions include transitions. Use transition actions if the actions on a state don't include one, or to add branching behavior to your state machine.

Transition Actions

- **In view** – Perform a transition based on whether the entity is in a camera's frustum.
- **Listen** – Perform a transition on receiving a system bus message on a channel.
- **Random transition** – Perform a random transition.
- **Transition** – Transition to a different state.
- **Transition on next frame** – Transition to a selected state on the next frame.
- **Wait** – Perform a transition after a specified amount of time, or a random amount of time between 0 seconds and a specified maximum number of seconds.

111

Scripting

Add scripts to your scene to update your scene based on user input or events. You can use scripts to access the DOM, create and modify entities with the Sumerian engine library, or use the AWS SDK for JavaScript to access AWS services and resources.

Note
Visit this guide's GitHub repo for a collection of useful sample scripts. Contributions are welcome!

To create a blank script

1. Open a scene in the Sumerian editor.

2. Create a blank asset by clicking the plus icon next to the default pack and then click **Script**. Select the pack name to see the icon.

3. Press j to open the text editor.

4. Choose the new script under documents. Use the pencil icon next to the script name to change its name.

The script template includes 7 methods and a parameters array. The methods correspond to a scene's lifecycle events and are called by the engine at the following times.

- `setup` – When scene playback starts.
- `fixedUpdate` – On every physics update.
- `update` – On every render frame.
- `lateUpdate` – Aafter calling all `update` methods in the scene.
- `enter` – On a state machine script action, when the state is entered.
- `exit` – On a state machine script action, when the state is exited.
- `cleanup` – When scene playback stops.

Reference documentation for the Sumerian engine library is available on the Sumerian website.

Topics

- Built-in Scripts
- The Context Object
- Parameters and Arguments
- External Dependencies
- Debugging

Built-in Scripts

The editor also has several built-in scripts that provide standard functionality like camera, keyboard, and mouse controls.

Camera scripts

- **Orbit camera control** – Lets the user orbit the scene by holding a mouse button and moving the mouse.
- **Orbit and pan control** – Lets the user orbit the scene with one mouse button and pan the camera with another.
- **Fly control** – Lets the user zoom and pan with the keyboard.
- **Axis-aligned camera control** – Move the camera to a fixed distance away on the X or Z axis.
- **Pan camera control** – Lets the user pan the camera by holding a mouse button and moving the mouse.
- **Mouse look control** – Lets the user look around by holding a mouse button and moving the mouse.
- **WASD control** – Lets the user walk around on the XZ plane with the keyboard.
- **Augmented reality camera script** – In an augmented reality (AR) scene, follow the device camera.

Object scripts

- **Button** – Lets the user click on an object to open a URL.
- **Pick and rotate** – Lets the user grab an object and manipulate its orientation.
- **Lens flare** – Generates a lens flare when the user looks at an object.

The Context Object

You can use the context object, `ctx` to store your script data during the script life time. The context is created upon setup() and cleared on cleanup() and is passed into all of the script functions. It has a the following properties:

Properties

- `entity` (https://content.sumerian.amazonaws.com/engine/latest/docs/Entity.html) – The entity to which the script is attached.
- `entityData` (`Object`) – A data object shared between all scripts on the entity.
- `activeCameraEntity` (https://content.sumerian.amazonaws.com/engine/latest/docs/Entity.html) – The currently active camera entity.
- `domElement` (`HTMLCanvasElement`) – The WebGL canvas element.
- `playTime` (`number`) – The elapsed time since scene start.
- `transitions` (`Object`) – Transition functions used to signal the success or failure of an **Execute script** action on a state machine.
- `viewportHeight` (`number`) – The height of the canvas.
- `viewportWidth` (`number`) – The width of the canvas.
- `world` (https://content.sumerian.amazonaws.com/engine/latest/docs/World.html) – The world object.
- `worldData` (`Object`) – A data object shared between all scripts in the world.

Some of the properties on `ctx` are shared between scripts. *entityData* is shared by all scripts on the entity and *worldData* is shared by all scripts. They are all initially empty, and can be used to store any kind of data

For example, if we'd like to define a property called *acceleration*, we could make it available on three levels:

```
1  // Only accessible to the script that defined the property
2  ctx.acceleration=9.82;
3
4  // Accessible to all scripts on the entity
5  ctx.entityData.acceleration=9.82;
6
7  // Accessible to all scripts
8  ctx.worldData.acceleration=9.82;
```

The built-in context properties also contain some convenience functions. For example, the `world` object lets you search for entities based on their tags. You can get all entities with a specific tag with `ctx.world.by.tag`:

```
1  var entities = ctx.world.by.tag('myTag');
```

Parameters and Arguments

Parameters let you create scripts that are customizable by adding fields to the script properties in the editor. For example, the following script defines a parameter named `Velocity` that takes 3 numbers (a `vec3` parameter).

```
1  var setup = function(args, ctx){
2      console.log(args.velocity);
3  };
4
5  var parameters = [
6    {
7      name : "Velocity",
8      key : "velocity",
9      type : "vec3",
10     default : [1,0,0]
11   }
12 ];
```

During the setup phase, the script reads the parameter values from the **args** object and prints them to the console.

When you add an instance of the above script to an entity, the editor shows a **Velocity** field that accepts three values and reflects the default value.

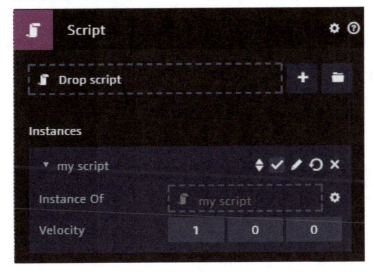

Parameter Format

Parameters are objects with the following required and optional fields.

Required fields

- **key** [string] – a unique key used to store and retrieve the parameter values in the **args** object.
- **type** [string] – the parameter type.
- **default** – the default value or values for the parameter.

Optional fields

- **name** [string] – the label for the parameter field shown on instances of the script. If you don't specify a name, the **key** is used to generate the label.
- **control** [string enum] – the control type.
  - **slider** – a slider control.

115

- `color` – a color wheel.
- `select` – a drop down listing the values in the `options` field.
- `jointSelector` – a drop down listing the joints on the animation component on the script's parent entity.
- `description` [string] – the description shown when you hover over the parameter.
- `options` [array] – an array of possible values for a `select` control.
- `min` and `max` [number] – the minimum and maximum values for an `int` or `float` parameter.
- `decimal` [number] – the number of significant digits for a `float` parameter.
- `step` [number] – the incremental value that `float` values snap to.
- `precision` [number] – the number of significant digits for `float` values.
- `exponential` [boolean] – set to `true` to distribute the values on a `slider` control logarithmically.

Parameter Types

The type property must be set to one of a few predefined strings, each corresponding to a type of parameter.

- `int` – Integer number variable (e.g. `1`).
- `float` – Number variable (e.g. `3.14`).
- `string` – String (e.g. `HelloGoo`).
- `boolean` – boolean (`true` or `false`).
- `vec2`, `vec3`, `vec4` – an array of 2, 3, or 4 numbers.
- `texture`, `sound`, `entity`, `camera`, `animation`, `json` – an asset of the specified type.

All types in action, including a sample script:

```
1  var parameters = [
2      {type: 'int', key: 'int', 'default': 1, description: 'Integer input'},
3      {type: 'float', key: 'float', 'default': 0.1, description: 'Float input'},
4      {type: 'string', key: 'string', 'default': 'Hello!', description: 'String input'},
5      {type: 'boolean', key: 'boolean', 'default': true, description: 'Checkbox'},
6      {type: 'vec2', key: 'vec2', 'default': [0, 0], description: 'Vector2 input'},
7      {type: 'vec3', key: 'vec3', 'default': [0, 0, 0], description: 'Vector3 input'},
8      {type: 'vec4', key: 'vec4', 'default': [0, 0, 0, 0], description: 'Vector4 input'},
9      {type: 'texture', key: 'texture', description: 'Texture asset drop area'},
10     {type: 'sound', key: 'sound', description: 'Sound asset drop area'},
11     {type: 'entity', key: 'entity', description: 'Entity drop area'},
12     {type: 'camera', key: 'camera', description: 'Camera drop down'},
13     {type: 'animation', key: 'animation', description: 'Animation state from the Animation
           component on the same entity'},
14     {type: 'json', key: 'json', description: 'JSON asset drop area'},
15     {type: 'float', control: 'slider', key: 'floatSlider', 'default': 10.1, min: 5, max: 15,
           exponential: false, decimal: 1, description: 'Float slider input'},
16     {type: 'int', control: 'slider', key: 'intSlider', 'default': 10, min: 5, max: 15,
           exponential: false, description: 'Integer slider input'},
17     {type: 'vec3', control: 'color', key: 'vec3Color', 'default': [1, 0, 0], description: 'RGB
           color input'},
18     {type: 'vec4', control: 'color', key: 'vec4Color', 'default': [1, 0, 0, 1], description: '
           RGBA color input'},
19     {type: 'string', control: 'select', key: 'select', 'default': 'a', options: ['a', 'b', 'c'],
           description: 'Dropdown/select'},
20     {type: 'int', control: 'jointSelector', key: 'jointSelector', description: 'Joint select
           from the animation component on a parent entity'}
21 ];
```

External Dependencies

If your script uses external JavaScript libraries from the web into your script, declare them in the **External resources** section of the text editor.

To declare external dependencies

1. Open a scene in the Sumerian editor.

2. Press J to open the text editor.

3. Choose a script asset in the **Documents** list.

4. Under **External resources**, enter a URL starting with // (excluding the protocol).

5. Click the plus icon to add the library to the list.

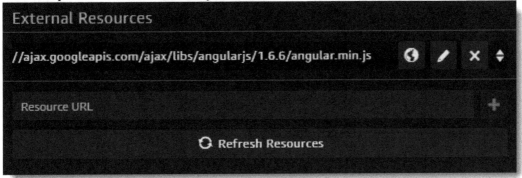

The editor loads libraries as soon as you add them to this list. To reload a library, choose **Refresh resources**. In your published scene, all dependencies are loaded and executed during the loading phase.

Debugging

To debug a script in the Sumerian editor, use the built in tools in your browser. In Google Chrome, open Developer Tools by pressing ALT-CMD-J on Mac or F12 on Windows.

Open the *Sources* panel at the top of Devtools. To the left you can see all scripts loaded in the browser. If you have a script in your scene, it will be listed in below *sumerian-custom-scripts*. Choose your script to view it.

The simplest way to start debugging a script is by adding a `debugger;` statement in your Custom Script in the editor. If you have Devtools open, and this statement is executed, Devtools will automatically go to the file and line where your statement is.

Troubleshooting Issues with Amazon Sumerian Scenes

This topic lists common errors and issues that you might encounter when using the Sumerian editor and player. If you find an issue that is not listed here, you can use the **Feedback** button on this page to report it.

Issue: (Chrome) Audio doesn't play in the Sumerian editor during playback.

Set the following flag to allow audio to play in the editor.

- **Autoplay policy: No user gesture is required.** – #autoplay-policy

To access Chrome flags, type chrome://flags into your search bar.

Issue: (Chrome) Can't enter virtual reality mode.

You may need to set the following flags to use virtual reality mode in Chrome.

- **WebVR** – #enable-webvr
- **Gamepad Extensions** – #enable-gamepad-extensions
- **Override software rendering list** – #override-software-rendering-list

To access Chrome flags, type chrome://flags into your search bar.

Issue: Browser uses the wrong GPU for hardware acceleration.

If you have multiple graphics cards, you may need to configure your system to use the right GPU for browser applications. For example, the NVIDIA control panel has an option named **target GPU** that you can set for each application.